WHEN
AIDS
Comes Home

ANSWERS TO THE MOST COMMONLY
ASKED QUESTIONS
What to Say, What to Do, and How to Live
with AIDS

Disclaimer

The accounts in this book are all based on true cases. Occasionally, to protect the privacy of the individuals involved, certain details have been altered.

Although this book contains medically reliable information, no part of it is intended as medical advice, nor should it be substituted for qualified medical care.

WHEN
AIDS
Comes Home

ANSWERS TO THE MOST COMMONLY
ASKED QUESTIONS
What to Say, What to Do, and How to Live
with AIDS

MIGNON M. ZYLSTRA
and DAVID BIEBEL

THOMAS NELSON PUBLISHERS
Nashville • Atlanta • London • Vancouver

Published in Nashville, Tennessee, by Thomas Nelson, Inc., and distributed in Canada by Word Communications, Ltd., Richmond, British Columbia, and in the United Kingdom by Word (UK), Ltd., Milton Keynes, England.

Unless otherwise noted, Scripture quotations are from the NEW KING JAMES VERSION of the Bible. Copyright © 1979, 1980, 1982, 1990, 1994, Thomas Nelson, Inc., Publishers.

Scripture quotations noted KJV are from The Holy Bible, KING JAMES VERSION.

Personal letters are used by permission.

Library of Congress Cataloging-in-Publication Data

Zylstra, Mignon
    When AIDS comes home : answers to the most commonly asked questions : what to say, what to do, and how to live with AIDS / Mignon Zylstra, With David Biebel.
        p. cm.
    Includes bibliographical references.
    ISBN 0-7852-7714-5
    1. AIDS (Disease)—Miscellanea. 2. AIDS (Disease)—Psychological aspects. 3. AIDS (Disease)—Social aspects. 4. AIDS (Disease)—Religious aspects—Christianity. I. Biebel, David B. II. Title.
RC607.A26Z95   1997
362.1'969792—dc20   96-28813
                                                             CIP

Printed in the United States of America
1 2 3 4 5 6 7 - 02 01 00 99 98 97 96

This book is dedicated to . . .

My precious son, Scott, who taught me how to live and how to die.

. . . my beloved husband, Bob, who supports and loves me and teaches me daily through his example how to love others.

. . . my darling daughters, Heidi and Wendy, and their husbands, David and Steve, who have listened so patiently and supported me on this journey.

. . . my three precious grandchildren, Brian Lee, Rachel Lynn, and Steven Tyler, who bring me so much joy.

I love you all!

. . . my Lord and Savior, Jesus Christ, who is my strength, my comfort, and my joy. He walks with me each step of the way, allowing me to always feel His presence, even in the darkest valleys.

Contents

Acknowledgments

Behind the scenes and pages of this book are those who encouraged us along in our journey and believed in us and the work we do.

I count myself blessed to have John Kingma, CPA; Chris Skinner, attorney; and Timothy Wezeman, D.D.S., as board members of *Support for the Journey*. Their encouragement, support, and many hours of work made it possible for us to become a nonprofit organization.

To Holly Halverson, Trudy Sundberg, Margaret Self, and Debbie Skinner, thank you for believing that this book should be written and for the gentle prodding I needed along the way.

I thank David Biebel for completing this project with me.

For their support throughout our journey with AIDS, I thank our families, especially both of our mothers, our brothers and sisters, nieces and nephews, aunts and uncles, and our many cousins. You all stood by, not always knowing what to say or do, but you were there.

Thank you, Aunt Stena, for deeding over a place in the Zylstra family burial plot so Scott could be buried at the foot of his great-grandfather, a final resting place with dignity.

For the transcription of many taped conversations, I thank Joni and Brian De Jong, and my dear daughter, Wendy Schierman, who also taught me how to turn my computer on!

For trusting me to share "our" story and encouraging me along the way, I thank you, Charly.

To LaVerne and Irv Rydberg and the Lamplighter Sunday School class, a big thank you for your continued prayers and support. You are a "class act"!

To Bud and Jeri Strom and family, and Kaye Olson, thank you for "cheering us on" from the beginning.

Thanks to Harlan Van Oort for being a special friend to Scott, and also to Bob and me. Your counsel, encouragement, and listening ear have made a difference for all of us.

To our many friends who showed us how much you cared and loved us, you are never forgotten.

We owe a debt of gratitude to Father Jack Tench for encouraging and guiding Scott toward spiritual restoration and loving and accepting him into his fold, and to the membership of St. Stephen's for ministering to Scott and us when we were so broken.

Thank you to Clint Webb for ministering to Scott and to us when Father Tench was on sabbatical.

We give thanks to God for Judge Patrick and for his love and faithfulness in ministering to Scott daily with devotions and prayer. He and Scott are now enjoying heaven together.

For ministering to us in the "early days," we thank Barbara and Bill Johnson and *Spatula Ministries*. Thanks also go to Deloris Richie for her support.

Our hearts are filled with gratitude for Drs. Siegel, Teays, Howe, and Knaack for the optimum medical care along with sensitivity and compassion they provided for Scott and to us as well.

To Janet Zylstra, Scott's aunt, who lovingly supported him and painted his portrait, which is truly a "gift from God."

Scott's original quilt panel, which goes with me wherever I speak, was created so beautifully by our neighbors, the Smiths. From our hearts, we thank you.

To a friend of Scott's, Kathy Nienhuis, for replicating the Smiths' quilt panel so Scott could be remembered on the National AIDS Memorial Quilt, thanks so much!

To the staff of Whidbey General Hospital, we will be eternally grateful for your love and support throughout Scott's illness. You cared for him like you would have for your own.

To all the "supporters" who give financially and of yourselves to *Support for the Journey*: You are loved and needed!

To all of the HIV-positive loved ones in our support groups, as well as those scattered near and far who are infected and affected, you continue to teach us so much.

And finally to my precious family, my daughters and their spouses, and my grandchildren, who are my inspiration, and my dearest Bob, who guided me along this project and is my greatest supporter, *I love you!*

Introduction:
How I Know What I Know

Some people get their HIV/AIDS* education in a classroom or a laboratory. I was thrust into new roles in a new world when our twenty-eight-year-old son, Scott, came home with AIDS in July 1988. Much of what I learned, Scott taught me. He taught me how to be strong, how to be brave, how to love unconditionally, how to forgive, how to laugh in the midst of fierce obstacles, and how to go on when life seems all but over.

Scott taught me about the struggles of homosexuality, about the depth of a mother's love, about a brutal disease that destroys the body but not the spirit and soul, about a son's love for his parents, and about losses and how we grieve them.

Scott taught me how to face death valiantly—even though he didn't want to die. He also taught me about faith—a deep, strong faith—and about leaning hard on the One who bears our burdens if we will give them to Him.

No one knew how long Scott would live when we took him home that summer to Oak Harbor, Washington. As a result of two recent near-fatal bouts—first Pneumocystis carinii pneumonia,* and then two weeks later, CMV* of the gut—Scott was so weak he could not take care of himself and death seemed near. Scott wept as he embraced his companion, Charly, and said good-bye.

I saved my own tears until later. I didn't know what our journey with AIDS would be like, but I did know one thing at that moment. My Scott needed me, and I needed to be with him. From that moment on, I would be his

*Asterisked terms are defined in the HIV/AIDS glossary in Appendix A.

primary caregiver. I had to be strong, or this dreaded disease would overwhelm us both.

In the few months prior, after learning Scott was HIV-positive,* I had read everything factual I could find about HIV/AIDS. I learned how we get HIV and how we don't get it. I read about opportunistic infections,* stages of HIV disease, and various treatments and their side effects.

But nothing prepared me for what was to come. The first days at home brought many issues, obstacles, and changes to our lives. I stepped in diarrhea twice on the bathroom floors and had to gently ask Scott to try to be careful. He was too weak and sick to realize this had happened. My dear son who was always so clean and conscientious. . . . Then Scott wanted to talk about dying issues at once, such as having a closed casket and not wanting to die at home. He also needed to find a church where he could worship and belong, since the leadership of our church had taken harsh action against him.

Another issue we faced was the knowledge that our family had brought the first known case of AIDS to our hometown. We live in a military town with a strong Dutch influence. AIDS did not belong there. And Scott's dad is the hospital administrator, so we brought AIDS to his dad's workplace.

We assured Scott he was safe and loved and protected in our home, but we could not answer for anyone else. There had been no time for a survey. In my heart of hearts, nothing beyond our family really mattered. We needed time to heal, time to love, time to say good-bye. Confronting others' prejudices would have to wait. There were gnawing questions that lurked in the recesses of my being. This was the toughest assignment I had ever had. Could I see it to the end? Could I be Scott's friend, his counselor, his nurse, his confidant? And most of all, I was still his mother. Could I help my son live and die with AIDS one day at a time? I was to learn that motherhood has a theology all its own. Its depths go far beyond anything we can imagine.

I was also to learn in a very real way that God's heart has room for all those who are infected and affected by HIV. It was a message we would be called to share.

You'll hear more about our journey through AIDS, which may be a lot like yours or that of someone you know, in the following chapters. You'll hear how Scott fought the good fight, and resolved a lot of issues before he succumbed to AIDS in 1989. You'll also hear how the experience took all of us deeper into faith and hope and love and other things that really matter.

After Scott's death, we established an organization called *Support for the Journey* to help people with AIDS (PWAs) and their loved ones face this devastating disease together. These friends, many of whom you'll meet in the following pages, represent a cross section of humanity. We have known PWAs who were single, married, adults, children, parents, siblings, men, women—heterosexuals, homosexuals, bisexuals. They came from various races, and all walks of life.

Many of these people were raised in Christian homes. Most of them are or were deeply interested in spiritual things. I tell them all, as I will tell you, that the reason we emerged from this ordeal *better* instead of *bitter* was not because of our strength, but because of strength that came from beyond ourselves, as a result of our relationship with God through faith.

From time to time I'll share more about that, for those who care to pursue it. But I promise not to preach. Rather, I'll try to live the message of love that my faith requires and which I am confident my Savior, Jesus, would practice if He were here.

HIV is a disease that impacts real people and their loved ones who must learn to face this together, because no one can face it alone. Since my primary calling is to walk with PWAs and their loved ones, I don't spend time condemning or excusing Scott or anyone else who may have acquired AIDS through immorality or irresponsibility. As you will see, Scott deeply regretted some of the choices he made that brought this disease and ultimately his untimely death. But I'll let him speak for himself.

Speaking for myself, I would say this. When I meet people with HIV/AIDS, it doesn't matter to me how they got it. All that matters is that they are human beings whom God loves so much and asks us to love too.

As we've worked with hundreds of PWAs and their families, we've noticed that certain issues keep surfacing, often in the form of questions. Because of this, we use those same questions as a framework, first for PWAs and then for their families and loved ones. At the end of each chapter you'll find practical suggestions for implementing the points you find most helpful.

I've written this book to guide and encourage others on a very difficult journey, not because our experience with AIDS was unique, but because the issues we faced are so common to PWAs and their loved ones. I believe that the lessons we've learned, by experience or by observation, can help you transform unbearable agony leading only toward despair into constructive sorrow that can lead toward deeper understandings of life and death and relationships. This understanding would not be possible if it weren't for the fact that AIDS has invaded your life and changed it forever.

AIDS Lesson 1:
People facing AIDS do better when they know what to expect on the journey. They do best when they don't have to find their way alone.

This is true of both the HIV infected and the caregiver. We'll start with the needs of the PWA.

PART
1

Issues Often Faced by People with AIDS (PWAs)

How Will I Tell My Parents?

1 For many people I've known who were living with AIDS, their primary concern after the initial shock of learning their HIV status was not "I'm going to die," but "How will I tell my parents?"

That's the way it was for Arianna, a former flight attendant. Arianna is a beautiful person, inside and out. When we travel together, her face and body cause heads to turn. But how those observers would shudder to think that this beautiful young woman has AIDS!

Arianna was shocked herself to find out she was HIV-positive. Living in Paris, about to be married, she and her fiancé decided to be tested because several of their friends had tested positive.

Once the results were confirmed, Arianna's thoughts immediately turned to her parents, who loved her dearly but lived so far away in the United States. She knew that the simple words "I am HIV-infected" would break their hearts and shatter their dreams for her. But she also knew they deserved to know the truth directly from her rather than through someone else. She enlisted her older brother's help. Together they visited their parents for the holidays and broke the news as gently as possible.

The problem is, no matter how many times you practice saying the awful phrase "I am HIV-positive," it always sounds less than gentle to those who hear you.

"It hit my parents like a truck," Arianna recalled, "and then my big, strong dad dissolved in tears."

But the net result was constructive. Now Arianna travels around this country, speaking to young people and corporations about the dangers of drug use and promiscuity. As she travels, her parents and extended family are her greatest supporters.

When Scott told us, he kept it simple too. I will never, never forget the day, the time, the setting, and how I felt when he said those words. It was July 23, 1988, 9:35 P.M., in room number 414, right across from the nurses' station on the fourth floor of Century City Hospital in California. Bob and I had rushed there from Washington because earlier in the day Scott's temperature had hit 106 degrees. It seemed possible that he might be dying.

"Mom and Dad," he said, "I have AIDS. My doctors have given me nine to twenty-four months to live."

I was shocked, but certainly no more shocked than when he had told us he was gay. If I was less shocked to hear the word *AIDS* than to hear the word *gay,* it was only because Scott already had told us that he was HIV-positive. Since learning that at the end of 1987, I had read everything factual I could get my hands on about HIV/AIDS. Consequently, my mind was somewhat prepared for this, though I hadn't expected it quite so soon.

In my mother's heart, however, something else happened—something that defies explanation on a purely human level. Instead of despair, there was peace. It wasn't surrender either. No. I hated the disease and what it was doing to Scott. I never did give in to it, though later I was forced to accept the inevitable reality that AIDS had won, at least on a physical level. But even from that first moment, as my emotions were perhaps somewhat numbed by shock, AIDS was unable to conquer me on a spiritual level. The same was true for Bob and Scott. As a result, AIDS was never able to truly beat us.

If you're not a Christian, you may want to label this reaction as shock, denial, or something else. But to us it was a supernatural gift, because instead of being totally devastated, we just wanted to hold Scott and comfort him and let him know that we loved him and that we would be there for him, whatever it took and no matter how long it lasted.

We talked for several hours that night, even though it was late. In the HIV/AIDS ward at Century City Hospital, the clock was never an issue. The important issue was healing and reconciliation with family and friends.

The staff looked after us with great care and sensitivity. They, and Scott, helped us understand all the equipment in the room and how it worked. There were many pumps and tubes and monitors. All hooked up to Scott.

Scott also told us that he had arranged a meeting for us the next day with his doctor, who would explain the prognosis and answer any of our questions. Even as our son struggled to overcome a nearly fatal bout of Pneumocystis carinii pneumonia, he had been thinking about us. That's the way he was—thoughtful, kind, gracious, sensitive—through his long struggle with AIDS.

Hearing the diagnosis that night changed my life forever. It also changed the way I related to Scott's homosexuality, and even the way I related to his companion, Charly, who truly cared for Scott too. When Scott first told us that he was gay, we had a very hard time. Our hope and prayer was that our son would leave the homosexual life behind.

However, once I knew that Scott had AIDS, all our

other concerns became secondary. We gave them to God and left it all to Him. At that moment, I gained a new freedom. I was free to love, leaving the judgment to God. But the urgency of Scott's situation forced me to face this reality: *Scott is who he is. We may not have him too much longer, so every moment is precious.*

In regard to Charly, the grief we shared during and after those days brought a whole new dimension to our relationship too. In the shadow of AIDS, we stood on common ground, equally powerless in some ways and in need of help from beyond ourselves. For five days we enjoyed Charly's hospitality (and that of his mother, with whom he lived) as Scott slowly recovered. We learned a lot about love during those days, not only ours for Scott, but ours for Charly too. Most importantly we learned lessons we might otherwise never have learned about God's love for all of us. As I focused on my own heritage, I realized that in the light of God's perfect righteousness, there was little doubt that all four of us stood equally in need of His forgiveness and grace.

All these things happened partly because Scott was so open with us. Of course, we didn't want to hear that he had AIDS, but it was through having to face reality, together, that the opportunity for reconciliation and a new beginning emerged.

AIDS Lesson 2:
Most parents prefer knowing if their son or daughter has AIDS, because for everyone involved, AIDS makes every moment more precious.

So far in this chapter, I've described two positive examples of how this very difficult issue was handled. I wish I could promise that if you approach it in a certain way, you will have a similar outcome. However, partly because AIDS so often comes from a lifestyle that many parents consider immoral or irresponsible, many PWAs have grown increasingly alienated and disconnected from their parents (and possibly their entire family) through the years. Thus, when they are forced by AIDS to turn toward home for help because there is nowhere else to go, the door may seem to be closed. The risk of having this perception confirmed, which would add the weight of rejection to the weight they are already carrying, may be one reason many PWAs struggle so over how to go about telling their parents.

Based on what I've witnessed, AIDS can mark the end of a relationship, or it can be an opportunity for renewal. Very seldom does it have a neutral effect, because this disease has a way of painting the choices involved in black and white. The main choice is: "Am I willing to invest the energy necessary in order for reconciliation to take place?" This applies to all the parties involved, but it usually falls to PWAs to seek the reconciliation, perhaps because they carry the weight of shame that this dreaded disease has now invaded their family circle. This isn't fair; it's just a fact.

Sometimes, even though they make sincere attempts, PWAs experience rejection. This is sad. So sad it breaks my heart every time I see it or hear about it.

One tragic case involved a man I called "Little Joel" because of his size. His symptoms were somewhat like our Scott had experienced; specifically, neuropathy* in his legs that caused him great pain and made him walk like a little old man.

While at a retreat for PWAs, we were sitting around a campfire one evening lighting candles for those who had died of AIDS and giving thanks for the positive things in our lives. During this time of sharing, Little Joel said, "I'm Joel, and I'm a born-again Christian. But besides that, the thing I'm most thankful for is my mom. I don't know what I'd do if I didn't have her. I've been getting sicker for awhile, and finally I couldn't take care of myself anymore. But she said I could come home. She said she would take care of me."

Later, when most of the others were still enjoying the campfire, I could see that Joel wasn't feeling good and was uncomfortable. I asked him, "Do you want to go back to the lodge?"

"I really do," he replied.

"Do you want me to go with you?" I asked.

"Yes," he said.

So off we went in the darkness, carrying a flashlight and the blanket. Joel was quite wobbly. In fact, I was more or less holding him up as we tried to follow that dark trail. What happened next is as vivid in my mind as if it happened yesterday. As we were walking, Joel stumbled and fell and we both went down. Here was a young man who needed my support. But I'm not a very big, strong person, so we ended up in a heap. It was, in a strange sort of way, a bonding situation.

After I helped him up and brushed him off, I said, as we kept walking, "Joel, I'm so glad you've got your mom. Whatever you do, cherish that relationship. Let your mom know how much you appreciate her and love her."

"Oh, I do," he said. "She knows that, I've told her."

"I'm proud of you. That's so important," I told him. "I think you've picked the most important person to be your greatest supporter."

"Yes, I have, and that's what counts," he said, emphatically.

As we approached the lodge, I inquired, "What about your dad?"

When I said the words, I had my arm around Joel, and I could feel his whole body stiffen up. He growled an obscenity.

"Oh, Joel, I'm sorry," I said.

"After I had AIDS, I figured I would try one more time to make contact with my dad," he said. "My parents are separated. But I wanted to reach out to him and see if we could have any type of relationship. So I called him and I told him I had AIDS. I thought maybe if he knew I was going to die that he'd make an effort. Do you know what his reply was to me? He said, 'Well, Joel, you play and you pay.'

"I'll never see or talk to him again."

When Little Joel died four months later, he had made peace with the rest of his family and his faith—all the things that were important to him. His family had a wonderful memorial service for him. But he had to let go of his dad. He knew that that couldn't be resolved, and he didn't have the energy to keep beating on that closed door. So he let it go.

It was sad, and not only for Little Joel. As a parent I know what goes on inside. That father must have some real unfinished business gnawing away at him; he never saw his son again. He told him, "You play, you pay." I have often wondered about that dad and what he is now dealing with.

I know of a father who committed suicide over his son's grave a year to the day after his son was buried. He went to the grave site and shot himself because he never dealt with the issues related to his son's death. Consequently, he could no longer live with himself.

AIDS Lesson 3:

Attempts at reconciliation are always worth the effort, even if they do not achieve the desired result, because dying in peace is far better than living with unresolvable hostility. Fair or unfair, it usually falls to the PWA to make the first move.

Suggestions for PWAs

1. Tell your parents directly, but as gently as possible, choosing a setting where they will be comfortable enough to express their emotions over the news.

2. Enlist a trusted family member or friend's support, inviting him or her to be present at the time to help answer questions or defuse, deflect, or even absorb negative emotions.

3. Expect rejection, hostility, or judgment, some of which will arise from the situation itself, but which may be directed toward you for a time.

4. Persist in your attempts at reconciliation. Your parents are heart-broken, hurt, and possibly embarrassed. They may choose to love you again, in a deeper way, if you never give up.

5. If all your attempts fail, let it go. You can only control your own side. Besides, there is a long battle looming that will demand all your energy. Perhaps as they see the way you face AIDS, they may have a change of heart.

Suggestions for Parents

1. Reach out and touch your son or daughter who has HIV/AIDS. A little hug goes a long, long way. Many hugs go even further. Don't worry. You can't get HIV from hugging.

2. After you recover from your initial shock, get educated about HIV/AIDS and caring for PWAs, since it may be your privilege to accompany your son or daughter on this journey, which no one should have to make alone.

3. Do not allow your words or actions to be driven by negative motivation from within (such as anger, shame, resentment, etc.) or from without (peer pressure, ostracism, judgment, etc.). All that matters now is that your child needs your help. Trust me, you will never regret providing that help, but you will regret withholding or refusing it.

4. If you are religious, don't let your religion get in the way. PWAs cannot atone for their sins (neither can the rest of us), though many religious people seem intent on forcing them to try. Therefore, practice grace and forgiveness by asking yourself, "What would Jesus do?"

5. Seize the opportunity that HIV/AIDS presents to make every moment count. The longer you wait to do this, the fewer moments you will have to count.

Why Should Anyone Risk Caring, Knowing It's a Dead End?

2 "Mignon, you know I'm going to die," Peter said. "You've been so good to me and we've grown so close. I hate to see you go through this again."

Most PWAs are very concerned for the pain their illness brings to others. This concern, mixed with the guilt and low self-esteem so many PWAs struggle with, produces in them a perception that since their days are numbered, any relationships, especially new relationships, are dead ends; therefore, *why bother?*

This was Peter's real concern. This sensitive young man was giving me a way out if I wanted out.

I didn't.

"Peter," I said, "when Scott died a little light went out inside of me. Part of me died and went to the grave with him. I experienced one kind of pain when he was born, and another kind of pain when he died. In both instances, I accepted the pain as part of being Scott's mother.

"With you it's different. I'm your friend. It's a choice I've made. When you're gone I'll remember you fondly, and I'll miss you very much. But you're not gone yet. So let's make the most of the time we have left."

When my dear friend Josh was getting sicker, he and I would have long conversations about his family. He felt sorry for what he was putting them through and because they would have to grieve. He said, "I'm not afraid to die. I know I'm going to heaven, but I'm so concerned for my elderly parents and brothers and sisters."

This reminded me of conversations Scott and I had fairly often.

One night I was kissing Scott good night when he was in the hospital. His body was warm due to a low-grade fever. I leaned my head next to his for awhile. I just seized the moment, wanting it to last forever. During those seconds, I wanted to be able to die when Scott did. Finally, I said, "Scott, Dad and I are traveling this journey with you every step. But you are the lucky one, because you get to take one last step into eternity, and we have to stay here."

Scott replied, "I know, Mom, and I worry about you." A tear rolled down my cheek, but I quickly brushed it away before it fell on Scott's face. I needed to be strong for my son.

Love filled that room. All the differences and misunderstandings were gone. Love prevailed: our love for each other, our love for God, and His love for us.

Remembering this, I told Josh I was going to miss him after he was gone, that he had become a very dear friend, and that the experience of being his friend had brought me greater joy than the fact of his dying had brought sadness.

He replied, "Thanks for telling me that, Mignon. I appreciate your honesty. You have been one of my best friends, and I'm glad that our friendship has been so real."

Josh then asked, "Do you ever hesitate becoming someone's friend, knowing that in a year or two he or she will die?"

"I can honestly say that I trust God to take what He

has called me to and to bless it," I said. "If I live in fear of what will happen, I could never reach out and love."

I'm amazed at how uncomfortable most people, including religious people, feel around death and the dying process—which is a big issue facing people HIV-infected and their loved ones. We carry on as though we will live on earth forever, that this life is the best and only important reality, even if we say we believe in a life hereafter.

Truthfully, heaven became more real for me during Scott's last days, when we cheered him on to die. We knew that he was ready in every way—spiritually, emotionally, mentally, and physically. We encouraged him toward his release. "Scott, go, go," we said. "Your mansion is ready. The welcome mat is out, and it is all decorated. There's a black Rolls Royce in the garage!"

Some of my more theological friends may question this. I don't mind. The main question is: Is eternity something we look forward to, or do we prefer this life because we can see it? To us, Scott's death wasn't a "dead end," but an opportunity to help him make the small step from what we call life into something bigger and better, beyond words and our ability to imagine.

When I have the privilege of accompanying friends like Josh or Peter right up to that doorway, it brings sadness on a human level, but on another level—in my soul—it brings joy.

PWAs and their caregivers must face this issue early on in order to overcome the temptation to withdraw from each other in the face of AIDS. As human beings, we want to avoid pain and increase our happiness as much as we possibly can. AIDS brings pain, or at least promises it in the future; the more emotion invested in the PWA, the more potential for pain when he or she dies. If we love a lot, we are going to grieve a lot.

Logic suggests (perhaps demands) that the way to protect ourselves is to withhold the emotional investment. Love, which operates in another realm and originates beyond ourselves, demands something else.

Here's how my coauthor expressed this dilemma poetically in his book *Jonathan, You Left Too Soon,* after his three-year-old son, Jonathan, died of an undiagnosed illness:

Dilemma

My boy, the joy had just begun,
But suddenly your life is done
And, stunned, I, lonely, wander on
Without you, an automaton.

I wonder, dare I love again,
Or was our loving all in vain,
A passing pleasure tinged with pain?
Am I to live, or just remain?

Tormented by the nagging fear
That one, once loved, will disappear,
Should I withdraw or venture near?
Is there an answer that is clear?

"Withdraw! Withhold!" my heart replies,
"To love again would be unwise!"
Yet something whispers otherwise,
That only loving satisfies,
Beautifies, or edifies.

AIDS Lesson 4:
AIDS will force you to choose to withdraw or love more deeply. Even if there were no eternity, loving would be better for everyone involved. Since eternity exists, however, loving more deeply has both present and future value. Take the risk.

But let me warn you. Truly loving a PWA or a caregiver who is a flawed, imperfect human being will prove impossible if you try to do it in your own power. I know I couldn't. As I told Josh, the single thing that takes me beyond my fears and ignorance is my sense of calling.

Had it not been for Scott's illness and death, I would probably never have gotten involved with individuals and families who struggle with this modern-day plague. I might have figured, like many others seem to, that this disease afflicts bad people, which does not include me or my family; therefore, I don't have to get involved. I would have probably gone on my way, trying just to catch as much happiness as possible for me and my family, oblivious to the needs of a growing segment of our society and humanity worldwide.

AIDS changed all that, and I am grateful. I don't mean I am grateful for AIDS, in general, or for the fact that Scott died of AIDS. But I am thankful that as a result of our experience with Scott's AIDS, we were shaken out of our self-centered complacency and thrust, totally, into a world of human hurt that our faith demanded we do something about.

I remember exactly the moment this happened. I was sitting in Scott's room in Century City Hospital during his second acute illness, only two weeks after his recovery from near death.

This time, although nine specialists were working on Scott, they still didn't know what was causing his temperature of more than 105 degrees. They told me that Scott could be dead before this infection was diagnosed (in those days it took several weeks to culture CMV, which is what it was). Here were some of the pioneers in AIDS work telling me that they *hoped* they were treating Scott with the right antibiotic.

It was one of the most difficult weeks of my life. Scott's temperature would go down a half degree and there would be a flicker of hope. Then it would go back up, and the crisis was in our faces again. Scott was too sick to talk to me. For the first three days of that week, he was totally incoherent, although I'm confident he knew I was there. Bob was at home, planning to come to L.A. over the weekend. Even though I had excellent support from the staff, I was feeling very alone.

I sat in a chair in the corner and looked at Scott lying on the bed. *He could be dying,* I thought. *Life has changed forever.*

The reality of this hit me with such force that I cried out: "God, this is too hard for me! I can't do this. I can't watch my son die."

Suddenly, as I sat there in tears, God's peace came over me as His Spirit personalized one of the Bible verses I had taught Scott and his sisters years earlier: *I know it is too hard for you, Mignon, but My strength is made perfect in your weakness* (2 Cor. 12:9).

I am weak, all right, I silently replied.

But then I heard something else as clearly as if God said it in person: *Mignon, there is a world out there that needs to know about My love. I want you to go and love them.*

I knew in my heart that the world He meant was the patients in those other fifteen rooms, none of whom had any family there to support them.

I knew what my response had to be. But I didn't bolt out of the chair and rush from room to room. I thought about it for awhile. I knew that walking into someone else's room uninvited was to invade his or her territory and to violate his or her right to privacy . . . both of which I was confident Jesus would never have done.

After some time, I stood to obey. The very first room I went into was the room that Scott had been in during his first visit to Century City. Jerry, the patient in that room, was staring at the ceiling. He was very sick. I prayed all across the hall. "God, I will go and be Your servant, but give me the wisdom and the words. Help me to say the right thing."

I didn't want to offend Jerry or to be driven out of the room. So I started by asking, "How is it going today?"

When I asked that, I put my hand on his blanket-covered leg, very lightly, not knowing whether he had pain in his legs. After that, he just started talking to me.

After we had talked for awhile, I said, "Jerry, I can see that this is a very lonely place, and that AIDS is a very lonely disease. Do you ever feel alone?"

"Sometimes," he said. "Sometimes it seems like no one loves me."

"Well," I said, "I just wanted to tell you that God loves you and that you are precious to Him."

Then I shared with him about how this experience was very hard for me as a mom, and the only way I could get through this was knowing that God cared about me and that He had His watchful eye on me and on Scott—that He loved Scott even more than I did.

"How do you know that?" Jerry asked. "How can you *really* know that?"

So I told him about my background, about growing up in a Christian home and going to Sunday school when I was a child, and about how I believed in God with all my heart and that was my faith.

"I want to believe it," he replied. "I went to Sunday school, too, when I was a kid. My parents sent me. But since then, I've just drifted."

The conversation was very relaxed after that; not forced at all, which was amazing, since I'd had no training in how to do this. But I think the real breakthrough occurred when I asked Jerry if there was anything I could do for him that would make it a better day for him.

"Yes," he said. "Would you rub my back?"

"Okay," I said, not really sure how to proceed. But I put the lotion on my hands and he rolled over on his side and I gave him the best back rub I knew how to give.

AIDS Lesson 5:

Because PWAs are often lonely, they need to know they are loved. This can be shown in many ways. One way we can demonstrate it is through touch.

The most important point, in terms of my own continuing involvement with PWAs, was that Jerry picked up on my offer to help him. This helped me. Without him, I wouldn't have known how valuable a back rub could be . . . or that God's grace really was sufficient for me in trying to creatively minister in this difficult situation. I went to Jerry's room not knowing what to say or do, or how it would go. When I was ready to leave, he wanted me to stay longer.

He could have said that he was really tired and that he didn't need anything, or that he needed to rest. But because he allowed me to help him, I went back to Scott's room convinced that not only *should* I do what had seemed impossible, but that I *could* do it, with God's help. I can truly say that He has never let me down from that day forward. That doesn't mean I have done everything right, but I have never felt like a failure, either.

By the time we left Century City, I had visited every patient on the floor. And all of the people involved there, including the staff, had started calling me "Mom." This was the beginning of a whole new era in my life. While Scott was still with us, I was "Mom" to him. Day and night for fourteen months I tried to do what I could. But after he died, I began to be a type of mom to others in the gay community, a risk I embraced because I knew how Scott had been treated unfairly, even unmercifully, at times, and I wanted to help these people see that the love of God still exists in this world for them.

But they have helped me see things more clearly too. As St. Francis of Assisi said, "In giving, we receive." Despite the sorrow, I receive a deep inner joy when I go to a person's memorial service. Inside my heart, I cherish the memories I have of that person, of hearing him or her say that Christ is his or her Savior. Often I feel a deep sense of relief that the person's suffering is over.

But the lessons I learn from PWAs are not just about dying. Many of them have taught me how to live; that I have so much baggage in my life compared to them. Their concerns are about the bare necessities: "What do I need to live today? I need all my medications. I need my one (or two or three or four) infusions a day. I need a place to live, a small apartment will do. I don't have to have a lot of anything because I won't be on this earth much longer."

Their perspective forces me to look at my life and think, *Mignon, you act like you're going to be here forever.* I'm a pack rat, and I have all these things, all kinds of stuff I really don't need in order to live one day at a time, which is all I have, just like them.

Suggestions for PWAs

1. Anticipate that you and your caregivers may want to withdraw because you can see an early end to the relationship. Fight this temptation. You're not gone yet. You can choose to love more deeply.

2. Realize that your caregivers may be afraid of death in general, and your dying in particular. They need your help to see that learning to die is part of learning to really live.

3. Accept help from others when it's offered, even if those offering it don't really know what to say or do. It's one way to give back to them and to prepare them to help others after you're gone.

4. If you think your life is a dead end, why not risk believing that death is a doorway between two realities, the one much bigger and better than the other? You have nothing to lose, and everything to gain.

Suggestions for Caregivers

1. Confront your fears honestly and openly, perhaps with the help of a friend or support group. Specifically, confront the fear that the more emotion you invest in your PWA, the more your heart will break when he or she dies. This is exactly what will happen, but you will never regret the investment.

2. Listen to the inner promptings you receive related to caring and loving. Don't let your weaknesses keep you from fulfilling them. God will help you if you simply ask Him to.

3. Touch your loved one. He or she needs that sense of personal connection to life. If possible, learn how to give a good back rub.

4. Learn whatever you can from your PWA, especially how to live one day at a time.

5. Give without expectation of return, but don't be surprised if you receive more than you give.

Do All Religious People Hate Me?

 David was born and raised in California. After his formal education, he went to work in the film industry. He entered Century City Hospital with CMV. Soon complications set in, and he never left the hospital until he died.

Before developing AIDS, David had been a very handsome and proud man, with beautiful, thick, black hair. By the time I met him, his hair was thin and lighter in color. The rest had fallen out because of his chemotherapy treatment. No matter who came to see him, he still tried to be as perfectly groomed as possible, despite large, dark KS lesions* that were on his body.

One day not long after receiving the "prompting" I mentioned in the last chapter, I paid David a visit. "Hi, David, how is it going?" I asked with a smile.

"Okay," he said. "How is Scott?"

"The same," I said. "His fever is still high. The doctors can't give me any hope that he will turn the corner."

David stared at me for a moment, then asked, "Mignon, how can you smile when Scott is so sick and you don't know if he is going to live?"

"Well," I hesitated, knowing David was Jewish. "For one thing, there was a time when our relationship was very strained, and I didn't even know where Scott was living. So I'm just happy to be here with him. Now we can heal the relationship and love each other. That's one reason."

I paused again. "But there's another reason, a bigger one. It's because I know Scott's life is in God's hands. I really have God's peace about this. As much as it hurts me, I feel His peace. I don't know how else to say it."

Then I asked David if he ever felt God's love.

"At times," he admitted, "I don't. I really don't."

That was as far as the conversation went that day. I didn't push it, nor did he. I figured we could talk again when he was ready.

A couple of days later, a boyhood friend of David's and his wife were standing in the hallway outside David's room, obviously very troubled. I didn't want to intrude, but on the AIDS floor at Century City Hospital a certain bonding naturally took place among all the people—patients, staff, visitors. We all faced something bigger than any one of us.

"How is it going with David?" I asked.

"Not well," was the reply. "We grew up together. We came all the way out here from Florida to visit, and he won't see us. He won't see anybody."

"I'm so sorry," I said. "I'm Scott's mom. His room is two doors down. I don't know why David won't see you, but I do know this is a dreadful disease that can be really tough on family and friends."

"Oh," they replied, "we know why he won't see us. He's depressed. He knows he won't live much longer, so he called the rabbi because he wanted to make peace with God.

"The rabbi came all right, but he had his own agenda,"

they continued. "He chastised David for the life he lived and gave David no peace or assurance. After he left, David shut the door and made it clear that no one could come in except the nurses."

A couple of days later, one of the nurses saw me in the hallway. "David doesn't want to be alone," she explained, "and I have other work to do. Would you be willing to go in and sit with him for awhile?"

I was scared to go into that room because for three days the door had been shut. What if he told me to get out?

"I'll be Your messenger, Lord," I prayed. "But You'll have to give me the right words and show me the right things to do."

I walked into David's room. "Hi," I said. "Sue asked if I would come in and sit with you for awhile." I didn't want him to think that I was presumptuously crossing the barrier that he had put up.

He gave me a faint smile and said, "Hi."

So I sat down in the chair and didn't say anything. I didn't want to do the wrong thing. And I did want him to know that I respected his privacy as well as his need to control things as much as possible. I wanted to be his guest, not an intruder.

After sitting for awhile in silence, I reached over and patted him lightly on the leg. This opened the door.

"Mignon," he asked, "would you rub my legs?"

He had his pajamas pulled up, and I could see the ugly, dark lesions on his body.

"I would love to rub your legs," I replied. I put some lotion on my hands, and I began rubbing his legs. As I did this I told him that God loved him, He loved Scott, He loved me, and that we were His children.

"I wish I could believe that," he said.

"You can," I replied. "It's just a matter of faith."

"I wish I had your faith," he said.

"That's okay," I assured him. "If you will go to God and ask Him to enlighten your heart, He will."

We didn't talk about it much more during that visit, but I visited David often until we left the hospital ten days later. I rubbed his legs sometimes. Other times we would just talk. Each time I would assure him that God loved him. I had to be very gentle since he had been so hurt by his rabbi.

Based on my work with hundreds of PWAs, one thing is very clear. The church's reaction, whether the PWA is Jewish, Roman Catholic, or Protestant, is an enormous issue for a vast majority of PWAs. Most of the gay men I've known have had some type of Christian background, including Sunday school or some other religious training. Many of these people are very spiritually sensitive. They want to deal with the spiritual issues related to their dying. They long to embrace the church in some form or another.

However, because many of them contracted the disease through homosexual activity, the church has condemned them. For some reason homosexuality is singled out as the greatest sin of all, which of course isn't true. I'm not saying that I understand all that homosexuality involves, or that I ever will, but I can say that God has helped me leap over that hurdle to just see PWAs, however they acquired the disease, as people in need of God's love.

AIDS Lesson 6:
Most people with AIDS are deeply spiritual. "Religious" people often despise or condemn PWAs. Thankfully, God, who isn't religious but purely spiritual, loves both PWAs *and* those who despise them.

I could tell you other stories about PWAs (and even their families) who, when they turned to the church in their darkest hour, found not acceptance and support, but rejection.

But instead of telling you about them, let me tell you a little more about Scott's experience. I'll never forget how he put it.

"Mom," Scott asked, "do they hate me?"

Scott knew that all Christians did not hate him, he just had a hard time finding those who would show him unconditional love right where he was. It was difficult for him to find Christians who would encourage him or even talk to him about the issues he was dealing with. When it comes to the area of homosexuality, the church becomes paralyzed. Add HIV/AIDS and you have a double whammy!

Scott struggled with homosexuality for years, asking God to take away these feelings. Scott was a sensitive Christian young man who testified openly of his faith. He knew how the church felt about homosexuality; therefore, he shared with no one the nature of his struggle. Scott heard people talk about "those queers and fairies," and the words that were spoken were very unkind, thus pushing him farther into the closet.

Scott's personal experience with church leadership was devastating. They chose to deal very harshly with him without any effort made toward restoration. Consequently, members in the church and community came to us grief-stricken and in shock over the insensitive way Scott had been treated. I heard Charles Swindoll say on his radio program, *Insight for Living*, "Once church leadership has lost its integrity and credibility it is next to impossible to get it back."

Scott could have been destroyed by this experience. Even though it shattered him, it did not shatter his faith. God's power was greater than that of man! Scott's faith was restored, but not immediately. Thankfully Scott's life as a

Christian had been in place for many years. His years of Christian education from early childhood through college and Bible school in England had deep roots, so deep in fact that man could not destroy his faith. The power of God in the life of His child was very evident.

So, when Scott came home, expecting to die, he needed to find another church where he could worship and belong. The answer was St. Stephen's Episcopal Church. For some time after he returned home, Scott couldn't attend services because he was too weak, but Father Tench and some of the laypeople would visit regularly, always bringing Communion. Then the day came when Scott was able to go to church in his wheelchair.

Scott's doctor met us outside and wheeled Scott in, a true picture of compassion. Bob and I sat in the pew and Scott was in his wheelchair at the end. Someone had covered the heat register closest to Scott, to keep the draft off him. Everyone was attentive to our needs.

As we began singing hymns, Scott began to weep. I reached for the tissues and handed them to Bob who handed them to Scott. Of course, I kept some for myself. As Bob and I fumbled around trying to follow a liturgy that was unfamiliar to us, a gentleman behind us reached over our shoulders and assisted us throughout the service.

When it was time for the giving of the peace (in the Episcopal church they hug or shake hands and say, "The peace of the Lord be with you," and you respond, "And also with you"), people from throughout the church came over to Scott and hugged him and greeted him.

Then it was time for the Communion. Scott did not have the strength to go up to the altar so Father Tench brought the Communion down to him. In this church they use the common cup, but no one stayed away from that cup even though they thought Scott had drunk from it. (He hadn't.)

The love and acceptance were feelings we had missed for a long time. Scott felt that he belonged, so he studied hard and was confirmed at St. Stephen's the following May, with all our local family members in attendance. That morning, Charly called Scott from California. Scott said, "Charly, this is my big day. This is the day I've been waiting for."

An interesting, divinely orchestrated twist happened when it was time for Scott's memorial service. We needed a larger church to hold it in than the Episcopal church Scott had joined earlier that year. So Bob talked to the pastor of our church, who agreed that we could have the memorial service there. The Episcopal cross was carried in, and people from the Episcopal church shared. Because Father Tench, the Episcopal priest, was on sabbatical, a Baptist pastor performed the service. It was ecumenical in a very positive sense.

By the time Scott had developed full-blown AIDS, I was the one who still carried some bitterness about the fact that when we needed our church family most, there were fractures in the relationship due to leadership decisions. One day when I must have expressed this, Scott said, "Mom, I feel sorry for them. I'm not angry. I just pity them, that this is where they are as Christians. But it's okay, I've forgiven and moved on."

In that one interchange, Scott taught me about forgiveness. If he had forgiven them, I certainly should do so too. My faith requires me to forgive.

AIDS Lesson 7:
People may hurt or disappoint you. But you're better off to forgive and get on with living the rest of your life.

Before I end this chapter, I have to say that I can see some promising things on the horizon. Certainly, there is still too much misunderstanding in the church, but that will change.

I mentioned earlier that a very big obstacle Scott faced when he came home was to find a church where he could worship and belong. This was not a small issue to Scott—he wanted to get his spiritual house in order. God led him in a beautiful way to a pastor and a congregation that embraced not only Scott, but Bob and me as well.

St. Stephen's Episcopal Church made Scott a part of its family, looking after his needs—not only spiritual, but physical and emotional.

A man named Judge Patrick, a member of St. Stephen's, came to read and pray with Scott daily. Others sent cards and visited. One couple took Bob and me out to dinner while Aunt Bea and Sherm sat with Scott. They wanted to help us. The highlight of the week was when they would bring Communion to the hospital room each Sunday. There in room twenty-four, the hospice room at Whidbey General Hospital, we could all be together. Scott's sister, Wendy, would join us as often as possible. Sometimes other family members would be with us, and they were always included. At these times we felt so close to each other and to God. What a gift that church gave to us! There was no judgment, no scrutiny, just praise and thanksgiving to God. In our helpless state we were welcomed and feasted at God's banquet table. The sacrifice had been made for each one of us by our Lord and Savior.

One weekday Scott was feeling somewhat anxious, something PWAs experience. Father Tench was on sabbatical, so Pastor Clint Webb from the Baptist church was covering the special needs for him. Scott said, "Mom, I would like to have Communion today." I told him we would try to arrange it. The secretary at St. Stephen's contacted Pastor Webb and he said he would be happy to do this.

When Pastor Webb arrived, he and Scott shook hands. Then Scott said, "I don't know if you know about me."

Pastor Webb said, "Yes, Father Tench told me about you." I was touched by Scott's humility. They continued to talk while I sat quietly in the corner.

After some time, Pastor Webb asked me if I would like to join them for Communion. I said I would. We first sang some songs around the bedside. Scott, who was a gifted singer, had little lung capacity left, but he sang the best he could. The last song we sang was "Jesus Loves Me." As we were singing, I thought, *This is the first song I taught my little boy, and the message of that song takes us to our dying day.*

Jesus Loves Me
by Anna B. Warner

Jesus loves me! this I know,
For the Bible tells me so;
Little ones to Him belong;
They are weak, but He is strong.

Jesus loves me! He who died
Heaven's gates to open wide;
He will wash away my sin,
Let His little child come in.

Jesus loves me! He will stay
Close beside me all the way;
Thou has bled and died for me,
I will henceforth live for Thee.

Yes, Jesus loves me!
Yes, Jesus loves me!
Yes, Jesus loves me!
The Bible tells me so.

Then it was time for Communion. We first partook of the bread, and then when it was time for the cup, we elevated Scott slightly, since he was weak. Pastor Webb took the cup and put it close to Scott's face and said, "Scott, because of this and what it represents, you are the richest man in the world!" I will never forget Scott's smile. A pastor gave him permission to feel like a "child of the King!" What a gift we were given that day! This memory, among many others, is kept sacred deep in my heart.

This demonstrates a few things: first, that not all Christians hate PWAs; second, that the church can respond in a positive way if its people are properly educated and prepared; and third, that one person can make a real difference, transforming a tragedy that could have been made worse by judgmental attitudes into one whose impact was diminished because it was shared, for "a sorrow shared is a sorrow diminished."

Suggestions for PWAs

1. Don't be surprised if you experience misunderstanding, judgment, or ostracism from religious sources. It isn't that they hate you; they just don't know how to love you the way God loves you.
2. Forgive these misguided people and get on with your own journey. You can't change them, but you can control the way you respond.
3. Find your spiritual support somewhere. Just as your body needs good nutrition during this journey, so your soul needs spiritual food.
4. Never give up on God just because people who claim to know Him let you down. The stakes are too high, and the time is too short.

Suggestions for Caregivers

1. If your PWA is judged or put down in the name of religion, help him or her to honestly process this, if possible. Don't deny it or let it fester. This will only hinder the PWA's personal peace.

2. Avoid taking up an offense on behalf of someone else, which can easily produce bitterness in you, and hinder your ability to be a helper.

3. If your PWA needs spiritual support, try to locate an appropriate support group and attend it together regularly.

4. Do what you can to prepare your church or synagogue for supporting a PWA through the development of a good HIV policy (Appendix C), appropriate education, and the networking of various resources. Nobody has to tell you what the church doesn't yet seem to grasp—that before long, AIDS will be everybody's problem, because somebody will bring it home, and then your religious friends will have to face issues they could constructively process if they were properly prepared.

Why Shouldn't I End This Now?

4

All her life, after being abused as a child, Betty struggled with self-destructive thoughts. I met her through a social worker one year before she died.

Even before Betty acquired HIV, she abused drugs and alcohol. Like so many others caught in addictive, compulsive behaviors, she may have been desperately trying to fill the hole in her heart with something or someone, even if just for a few minutes. Or maybe she was simply trying to escape the pain.

After learning she was HIV-positive, Betty's substance abuse intensified, which clouded her ability to realize how much her husband and children (and many others, including me) cared about her. No matter what anyone said, the only voice Betty could hear was the increasing demand of her despair. *You are a burden to everyone, and it will only get worse. You're going to die a slow, horrible death, so do everyone a favor and take yourself out. The sooner the better.*

Finally, she gave in, overdosing on prescription medications.

AIDS Lesson 8:

Whatever your emotional weaknesses are, HIV infection will likely magnify them. The temptation is to bail out, but this dynamic can be an opportunity from which to learn and grow.

Betty lived two hours from me, so I didn't see her often. I put her in touch with other women living with HIV. They supported her as much as she would allow. I chastised myself for some time, thinking I had failed her in some way. But finally I realized that anyone who really wants to commit suicide can be successful. In reality, there was nothing I, nor anyone else, could have done that we didn't try to do.

Nobody knows for sure how many HIV-infected people take their own lives. But based on my observations, I would say that most people who face dying from this disease probably consider suicide at one point or another in their journey. This, rather than being a character flaw, is just one expression of the major depression most PWAs (and their caregivers) must work through in order to find peace and joy again.

Charly told us that after Scott learned he was HIV-positive, but before he was diagnosed with AIDS, he had talked about going to Holland, the land of our ancestors, where euthanasia is legal, to "get it over with."

But, like most of the PWAs I've known, after Scott actually developed AIDS (and had almost died of Pneumocystis), he seemed to discover a new peace about himself and what was ahead. Instead of suicidal thoughts, he seemed to want to make the most of whatever time he might have remaining.

I've seen a similar pattern several times, though in some cases it has taken a trip to death's very door to convince the suicidal person that living with HIV as fully as possible is preferable to death at one's own hand.

Bill was in medical school but had to drop out when HIV got the best of him. He was a very handsome man, long and lean. He had that "five o'clock shadow" beard, and eyes that were beautiful and piercing. When Bill looked at you, you felt as though he were looking into your soul! He never seemed to glance at anyone; rather, he *gazed* upon you. More than once, it froze people in their tracks.

I met Bill soon after Scott died. Often Bill would pull himself inward, and it was difficult to know what was really going on. We had a close relationship, but he had a hard time talking about how he really felt.

Then I heard that Bill had tried to take his life but had survived. I went to see him, and found him to be a changed person—more open, more positive. His dad had come from another state, and as the three of us talked, Bill said, "I will never try to take my life again."

"Why do you say that, son?" his father asked.

"Because it was very, very dark," Bill replied, "and I did not see the Light."

Bill came to know Christ after that experience. He talked about this many times with me before he died. His near-death experience had helped him find a wonderful peace with God. I would often sing to him using background tapes. One of his favorite songs was "There Is a Savior." He looked forward to heaven where the Light is bright and beautiful.

I first met Joe shortly after he had tried to take his life. He shared with me how he felt that no one cared about him anymore. He felt rejected by his family and his church. He felt God didn't love him either, so he might as well end it all. He took an overdose of drugs, but not enough to kill him.

It took Joe some time to realize and understand God's love for him. He had been wounded, and restoration took time. We first just loved him by making personal contact, phone calls, bringing food, and spending time with him. Slowly he began healing. He asked many theological questions that challenged me. For some I had no answers, and I told him so. But that was okay, with him and with me. What Joe needed most wasn't theological knowledge, but someone to walk with him on his journey. He slowly accepted that God's love, unlike people's love, is steadfast.

AIDS Lesson 9:
Soon after you discover you are HIV-positive, you may be tempted to take your own life. Don't, for if you will give yourself time to adjust to living with HIV, you will probably change your mind, and choose to live as fully as possible.

This transition takes time, but it takes more than time, for time alone cannot heal or change anything. Telling the truth to yourself and others (and even to God, which can be the most difficult of all), as often and as long as it takes, however, can bring significant personal growth and relational healing. This process is called "grief work," for a good reason: It is work, and it is about moving with and beyond our grief.

You may be familiar with the work of Dr. Elisabeth Kübler-Ross, who was a pioneer in the studies on death and dying. Dr. Kübler-Ross identified five stages in the grief process. These stages, which are common to both those who are dying and their caregivers, are: denial and isolation, anger, bargaining, depression, and acceptance.[1]

When Dr. Kübler-Ross set out to study this subject, she inquired about who in the hospital was dying. She was told that *no one* there was dying. Obviously, the caregivers had a problem with denial. Dr. Kübler-Ross's work opened up this whole arena, giving terminally ill people and those who cared for them permission to face and deal with reality, which is the only way to begin the process of inner healing and renewal that can happen even when a person's body is wasting away. In the New Testament the apostle Paul wrote about this: "Therefore we do not lose heart," he said. "Even though our outward man is perishing, yet the inward man is being renewed day by day" (2 Cor. 4:16).

I know this possibility may sound incredible, especially if you just learned that you are HIV-positive. But I assure you, based on our experience with Scott and my observations of many other PWAs, for some people the time when they are most whole and at peace is just before they die.

Perhaps this process of grieving is more focused when AIDS is involved because with AIDS, there is no known cure. (At the moment, this is the reality, but of course I hope this will change. There *are* some promising drugs available today, specifically protease inhibitors.*) You've heard that for a person who is dying, his whole life may flash before his eyes. This happens for PWAs too, but in slow motion. AIDS is slow-motion living and dying, which gives PWAs months, even years, to think.

I wish I'd known when Scott was sick what I know now about helping people process their dying. He would withdraw somewhere within himself and become very quiet, sometimes for hours at a time. Day after day he would lie on the sofa in the family room on double egg-crate cushions with sheets over them for comfort. In my mind, I can still see him lying there. His immune system was so compromised that he didn't have the energy to do anything except lie there in the silence and think.

I'd come downstairs and ask, "Scott, do you want the television on?"

"No, Mom."

"Do you want to listen to tapes?"

"No, Mom."

"Do you want the radio on?"

"No, Mom. I just have to think."

This interchange occurred many times during his illness.

I knew he was depressed, and that hurt me terribly. Every part of my mother's love longed for Scott to have some little glimmer of happiness, even though he was so sick.

When he would get really bad I'd think, *Okay now, I can't let this black cloud hit me because I'm the mother.*

But I was very, very sensitive to what he was going through and allowed him to process his situation. On the other hand I knew that if I allowed every one of his moods to affect me I probably couldn't be as supportive to him as I needed to be. So I tried to be strong.

I'm confident that during all those hours Scott was grieving the decisions and choices he had made in his life that had brought him to this point. I'd leave him for an hour because that's what he wanted—just to think. Maybe he was thinking about dying, maybe he was doing business with God, I don't know.

Sometimes I'd come back an hour later and ask, "How are you doing?"

"Fine," he would say, though that was obviously not true, at least the way I would define "fine."

But I didn't know how to help him. I didn't want to pry and get him upset with me, because we had to stay together. Neither of us could face AIDS alone. With someone else it would probably be easier. In fact, with many others, it has been easier to help them express how they really feel through asking them open-ended questions.

Sometimes I would just sit with Scott and rub his legs.

"Mom," he would ask, "why did I do the things I did?"

I don't know how many times he asked me that, or how many times I answered, "I don't know, Scott." I didn't know what to say, but his question gave me a peek into what he was thinking.

His absorption in the past broke my heart, but not just because of the failure he felt. I resented the past because it was also stealing our present, moment by moment, day by day.

If I had it all to do over again, I would try to help him talk about it. I would get him involved in a support group. But we were alone, with no support group. We did the best we could.

Also, I would let him see more of my tears. I felt that I had to be strong for him and I hid my tears. He'd walk through the room like a weak old man and I'd go upstairs and cry. But I never came down until I was dry-eyed and able to face him again. I didn't want him to feel guilty that he was causing us so much sadness.

Now that I've worked with many people facing similar issues, I can see how it might have helped to simply admit, "Yes, we are sad, Scott. Sad for us and sad for you. In any case, we forgive you, because we love you, and nothing you have done or might do in the future could possibly change that."

This commitment and support was there, and we expressed it by staying with Scott through the whole journey, right to the end.

I'm confident he knew this, but I wish we had talked about it more. However, I do think that knowing we were there for him, no matter what, provided the safe emotional environment Scott needed in order to move beyond his initial despair toward resolution and peace.

AIDS Lesson 10:

Some things are very difficult for PWAs to discuss with their families (and vice versa). But if you will courageously choose to probe these issues together (with the help of a group or a third party), you may be able to proceed more quickly with the grief process.

Grieving is hard, hard work. But it's worth the effort, because on the other side of the process is joy, which is far more substantial than happiness. (Happiness is dependent on circumstances—joy is not.) Depression, and the suicidal thoughts with which it bombards our minds, is part of the process. There's no way around it, but there is a way through it.

Mignon Zylstra

Suggestions for PWAs and Their Caregivers

1. Remember that grief is part of being human, but it doesn't have to beat you. If you expect to experience the different phases such as anger, denial, depression, and so forth you will not feel so lost, overwhelmed, or disappointed with yourself or others involved.

2. Find a way to express how you feel. Someone has said that depression is frozen rage. If you can find a way to safely unfreeze and express this anger, you will not be as depressed. If you can do this with the help of a close friend or professional counselor, you may find it easier to harness the energy involved for positive growth.

3. Cry when you need to, and as long as you need to . . . until there are no more tears. Some people think that big boys and girls don't cry, but this is a lie. Real people cry because they feel deeply, sometimes so deeply they can't put their sorrow into words. Jesus wept; David (the psalmist) wept; the prophets Jeremiah, Isaiah, and Daniel wept. Real helpers weep with those who weep. It's part of sharing life's deepest moments.

4. Always be honest with yourself and true to yourself. People may try to manipulate you into saying or doing the "right thing," which would force you to lie or pretend. Don't give in. Integrity is crucial. It was one of the most important qualities to the Old Testament character, Job, whose sufferings are recorded in the Bible book that bears his name. His "friends" cajoled, accused, and otherwise beat on him emotionally, but he never exchanged his integrity for the promise of their acceptance.

5. Realize that deep sorrow affects all your faculties, including the ability to make decisions and formulate sound judgments. Because human beings are comprised of body, soul, and spirit, when one part is hurting, every part suffers. This is why it is so crucial in your search for reintegration or wholeness that you resolve as many of the issues blocking your pathway as soon as possible, whether those issues be physical, intellectual, volitional, emotional, sociological, or spiritual.

6. Affirm faith whenever possible. The wonderful thing about the

Scriptures is that they reflect feelings PWAs and their caregivers experience. These feelings are common to people who have made the journey through pain in their own way. For example, Psalm 55:4–6 captures the way many PWAs feel at times:

My heart is severely pained within me,
And the terrors of death have fallen upon me.
Fearfulness and trembling have come upon me,
And horror has overwhelmed me.
So I said, "Oh, that I had wings like a dove!
I would fly away and be at rest."

For me, many Scriptures were helpful, especially this:

Fear not, for I have redeemed you;
I have called you by your name;
You are Mine.
When you pass through the waters, I will be with you;
And through the rivers, they shall not overflow you. (Is. 43:1–2)

7. If you struggle with suicidal thoughts, make sure you tell your counselor or trusted friend. If you have been making plans about how you might do this, please . . . please . . . please . . . tell your physician. There are medications that can help. And there are people who care. Don't believe the lie that your life has no value. Regardless of how old you are when you die, the ultimate measure of your life will not be its length but its depth; not the number of your achievements but the quality of your relationships.

8. Ask yourself, "How do I want to be remembered?" Then project yourself from the present to your death and ask yourself, "What can I still do to ensure that I will be recalled the way I hope to be recalled?" (Note: PWAs can do this more realistically than most people.) Then do it . . . with all your heart and soul, until you can't do it anymore. If you adopt this perspective, you will have a lot less

time for depression than you do now.

My friend, Arianna, is losing her eyesight, so she has had to give up driving. And she had to sell her beautiful little sports car. She has a big adjustment to make but keeps going because there are too many people out there, especially students, who need to hear what only Arianna can say in a way that will cut through their self-deception that HIV disease can't possibly ever happen to them. "It can," she says. "I am living, and dying, proof."

What Should I Expect?

5

I was at a retreat for people living with AIDS sponsored by a mainline denomination. I was there because I was a member of the retreat staff. Many of the people attending were in late-stage AIDS.

An emaciated young man named John came up to me and asked if we could talk alone. I said, "Of course we can." We sat down in a quiet corner of the Gathering Room and he began to talk. He was so frightened, and much of it seemed to stem from his lack of knowledge of HIV. His big concern at that time was MAC.*

"Mignon, did Scott have MAC?" John asked. "I'm so worried. I think I have it."

"Have you been tested for MAC?" I asked.

He replied, "No, I'm afraid to find out."

We talked for a long time about the disease, his fears, and why it is important to be informed and to have a good relationship with your doctor. I shared with him some of our experiences and how we coped.

When Scott and I left Century City Hospital to come home, the nurses gave us each a copy of *AIDS: A Self-Care*

Manual.[1] I went on to tell my new friend, John, that whenever Scott would have some different symptom, we would go to what we called *The Blue Book* (because this book was blue in color). We would pour through the pages trying to find out what might be going on. (We did this because we couldn't call the doctor for every little problem. We had an understanding with Scott's doctors that we were to call them if Scott's temperature was 103 degrees or higher.) *The Blue Book* provided us with a great deal of factual information, and many times it gave us clues as to what might be going on and what we could do. Sometimes we got our answer and we would be so pleased with our research. At that time resources were somewhat limited for the layperson. Now, though, both libraries and bookstores carry helpful books on everything from AIDS and ethics, AIDS and caregiving, and AIDS facts and issues, to AIDS, the spiritual dilemma.

John felt much better after our initial talk. He needed someone he could confide in. I felt privileged. Later, his suspicions were confirmed. He did have MAC. I never cease to be amazed at how "in tune" people with HIV become with their bodies.

The reason I start this chapter with this story is that scores of times over the past several years PWAs have asked me questions such as "Did Scott have seizures? Did Scott have MAC? Did Scott have CMV? Did Scott have neuropathy? Did Scott have PCP? Did Scott have KS lesions?"

Usually when this happens, I believe they're asking about a particular infection in the constellation of peculiar infections that result from HIV because they are personally experiencing symptoms of that illness, and they want someone who has been there to level with them about what to expect.

You might expect doctors to be the best sources of this information, but based on what I've observed, I'd say that most PWAs (and their caregivers) get much of their information about what to expect from something they've read or heard from someone who has been there. Support groups are an excellent place to exchange information and learn more about the disease.

I believe I understand why medical professionals may not properly prepare PWAs (and their caregivers) for all the possibilities. One of several reasons is that while people with HIV/AIDS do share a certain broad range of illnesses and symptoms, the disease causes a decline in each individual's health at a somewhat unpredictable rate and in a more unpredictable manner than doctors are used to dealing with. In other words, doctors may know a lot about HIV/AIDS and its management in a general sense, but they cannot predict with much certainty what course the disease will take for each individual PWA. Another reason is that too much information could be very alarming to the PWAs and their loved ones.

Additionally, after treating the patient's current symptoms with whatever medication works best, the doctor knows that the PWA will not recover as patients with other diseases usually do. Instead, he or she will be attacked by another infection sometime later which will further wear down his or her immune system, leaving the patient even more susceptible. Many doctors find this frustrating, since they really want to facilitate healing and the restoration of health, and AIDS is one of the few diseases that defies this.

Of course PWAs and their caregivers want their doctors to tell them the truth, but I can understand why many physicians may tend to reveal only what PWAs and their caregivers need to know in order to face the next phase of the disease. As I see it, this is consistent with the Bible verse about "speaking the truth in love," which means that when the speaker truly cares about the hearer, what is shared will be suited to the hearer's situation and needs, with a goal of encouragement versus dismay.

When Scott received his AIDS diagnosis, suppose the doctor had said: "Well, Scott, in the next nine to twenty-four months you will experience a gradual decline in your health during which you will face a progression of increasingly more difficult-to-treat complications, some of which will be painful and some of which will be disfiguring. You will always be tired. You may never feel good again. You may waste away slowly, regardless of how much you eat. When you need most to eat, you may find that you have no appetite, even for your favorite foods. You will have a constant fever and sometimes chills. You will have recurring and sometimes uncontrollable diarrhea and nausea not only from AIDS but also from the medications you will take in order to live a little longer. You will probably have seizures and possibly develop dementia* to the point where you are totally dependent on others, wearing diapers, and unable to walk or feed yourself. You may go blind. You will probably die a slow, excruciating, painful death which no one will be able to do anything to prevent."

Had our doctor said this to Scott (and us), you can imagine how our morale would have been affected. Instead, our medical consultants leveled with us when we asked for information, giving us enough to face what was happening at the time, but not so much that we became so totally overwhelmed or discouraged that we gave up.

AIDS Lesson 11:

You will probably acquire much of your knowledge about what to expect in your journey with HIV/AIDS from other PWAs and experienced caregivers. However, I suggest that you get your medical advice from qualified sources who will level with you.

Beyond the constellation of unpredictable physical symptoms, PWAs and their caregivers can expect to face a more predictable constellation of sociological, emotional, and spiritual issues. Preparing for these is as important as worrying about what your next physical problem may be, because while you can't do much to control the latter, you can exert control over your relationships, your feelings, and your spiritual orientation with the result that you will have more energy available to fight HIV's progression in your body.

Sociologically speaking, PWAs are often despised, rejected, and ostracized like the lepers of biblical times, regardless of how they acquired the disease. I could give many examples, none of which would surprise PWAs (or caregivers) reading this book. I know of PWAs who have lost jobs (along with their medical insurance), been evicted from their apartments, or even forced to move to another community simply because of HIV. Most of this comes from ignorance and fear, but sometimes it arises from a judgmental attitude that is directed toward the PWA and his or her caregiver.

My coauthor knows a former pastor in a midwestern city whose wife died of AIDS, which she acquired through a blood transfusion. The husband, his life and dreams shattered, also experienced rejection and ultimately ostracism because the church's simplistic theology could not accommodate the idea that bad things happen to good people, or that physical healing does not occur in every case, regardless of the quality or amount of one's faith.

Jesus found this type of sanctimonious attitude particularly distasteful in the religious bigots of His day. Beyond that, He specifically condemned turning one's back on those in need. "Assuredly, I say to you, inasmuch as you did not do it [feed the hungry, give drink to the thirsty, treat strangers hospitably, clothe the naked, and visit prisoners] to one of the least of these, you did not do it to Me" (Matt. 25:45).

How refreshing it is, therefore, to have an experience like we did with one of Scott's friends, Pastor Harlan Van Oort and his wife, Pat. Scott and I had traveled to Yakima so Scott could be interviewed about living with AIDS on a television program called *The Arena.* We had a wonderful visit, during which we spent some time at the Van Oort's home where Scott played with Elizabeth, their little girl. Harlan and Pat seemed so relaxed about it all. They seemed not to have any fears about HIV when Scott held little Elizabeth.

But something more surprising happened when Scott and I and the Van Oorts went out for dinner at an Italian restaurant. Scott loved food. But his stomach could no longer tolerate much, so pasta seemed the best choice.

The food on the menu sounded so good and it was prepared very tastily, but when it got right down to it, Scott could only eat a very little. The waitress, not knowing Scott's problem, asked, "Sir, is everything okay?"

"Yes," he replied, "the food is just great."

A little while later she asked him if everything was okay.

"Yes," he said, "I'm just not hungry."

"Would you like a doggie bag to take the rest home?" she asked.

"No," Scott said, "we're from out of town."

But Pat insisted, "Don't throw that away. We will take it home. One of us will eat it."

In that one statement, Pat expressed her acceptance and understanding more than almost anybody else did during Scott's entire illness. I'm the type that never drinks from the same glass as another person, healthy or not. But here was food that Scott had touched, and Pat was going to take it home for them to enjoy later.

AIDS Lesson 12:
Some people will make you feel like a leper. But others will make you feel like the leper that Jesus touched—accepted, a person of worth. When the first happens, ignore it. Only God can change people with attitudes like that. Let Him deal with them in His way. When the second happens, be thankful.

Over the long haul, however, the most daunting challenges come not from the disease itself, or even from other people, but from within the emotional and spiritual realms, which often seem to run together, even though they are separate.

In terms of emotions, AIDS has a way of testing every strength and exacerbating every weakness, like water when it freezes in the crack of a boulder, forcing it open for all the world to see. Since people differ in the way they're put together emotionally and how they're trained, the range of emotions associated with AIDS is quite broad. Therefore, I couldn't hope to touch every possibility even in several chapters. So I'd like to focus on these five: humiliation, anger, guilt, loneliness, and fear.

Based on his observation of the way other PWAs had died, Scott knew what he faced, particularly how humiliating it might be toward the end. In fact he told his doctors that he didn't want to die at home because he didn't want his mom to look at that place and recall his death.

Looking back, I appreciate his concern, because there

were many times during our journey with AIDS that our roles did regress, a situation that was highly distressful for me. I've already mentioned the situation with diarrhea on the rug. Later other medical crises caused him to lose control. I finally had to tell him, "Scott, I don't know how to say this, but I don't want you to lock the door anymore when you use the bathroom. If you happened to have a seizure in there and I couldn't open the door—this could be bad."

Here I was talking to my twenty-nine-year-old son, whose privacy as a man I wanted to respect, as if he were a little boy again, saying, "We have to be careful, Scott." I was feeling so much responsibility.

The moment stuck with me as a milestone in our journey, because I knew that from then on Scott could not be left alone. I'm sure this was humiliating for him, though he never said so. The positive result of humiliation, if you move with it instead of resisting, is humility, an attitude I saw develop in Scott and many of my dear friends as the disease forced their increasing dependence on others.

Anger is another common emotion for PWAs and their caregivers. As you recall, this is the first of Dr. Kübler-Ross's stages of grieving. Anger is a natural reaction when things seem unfair, which AIDS certainly is. Nobody deserves to contract HIV, although if they have constantly put themselves at risk, they ought not be totally surprised at the natural consequence of irresponsible behavior.

I've met some outwardly angry PWAs, though by the time I became involved with them and their families, the rage they harbored had turned inward to become depression, which I addressed earlier.

Interestingly, the angriest person I've met so far was the mother of a PWA. I'll never forget the first time we met.

I asked her if she had any church affiliation to give her support.

"I want you to know that I believe the Bible is the cruelest book ever written," she replied, "and St. Paul's writings are d—n mean, and you know yourself Jesus Christ was a homosexual."

You'll have to read chapter 10 to find out how I responded. But I will say this here: This woman had no support and had younger children at home. She needed a sounding board, and I was it. By the time her son Bailey died, she was learning to direct that energy more positively.

Guilt is also a major problem for PWAs, particularly those with religious backgrounds whose illness has come through promiscuity.

I'll never forget the words Brian said to me: "Mignon, I feel so guilty."

Brian came from a strong Roman Catholic family. He struggled for years with homosexual inclinations and remained celibate most of his life. As we became close friends, he shared with me that he had only "acted out" these inclinations twice, both times in a bathhouse in the early '80s. As Brian's health declined, spiritual matters were of utmost importance to him. He wanted to get things right between himself and God. We spent hours going over and over God's plan for us. I shared with him John 10:27–30:

> *My sheep hear My voice, and I know them, and they follow Me. And I give them eternal life, and they shall never perish; neither shall anyone snatch them out of My hand. My Father, who has given them to Me, is greater than all; and no one is able to snatch them out of My Father's hand. I and My Father are one.*

These words brought great comfort and assurance to Brian. He had been told by his church that he would go to hell, and he longed to hear about God's amazing grace. I also shared 2 Timothy 1:12, "For I know whom I have believed and am persuaded that He is able to keep what I have committed to Him until that Day."

Brian thanked me many times for sharing God's good news with him. He would tell me about his bedtime prayers. They were sweet and childlike and, I believe, precious to God. God extends His forgiveness to all who come penitently before Him through faith in Christ. Guilt is a terrible burden, but it can also be the route to finding peace with God.

Loneliness is also a major problem for most PWAs and their caregivers. I know it was very hard for Brian to have to face what he was facing without much support. The isolation many PWAs and their caregivers experience can lead to a sense of loneliness, even abandonment, at a time when companionship is absolutely essential someone to be there, someone to share the silence, someone to share the pain, someone to hold them.

The day Scott found out there was HIV involvement in his brain was one of those days when I just held him. He had had two grand mal seizures and was having further tests. The report came back: They were HIV-related. As test after test showed that HIV was attacking different parts of his body, it was difficult for all of us, but especially for Scott. He had no one else to talk to who was HIV-infected. There were only Bob and me, and I felt like I was letting him down by not having something comforting to say. All we could do was hold each other.

When Scott was in the hospital I would spend most of the day with him there. Some days we would engage in great conversations, but other days were quieter. When I would leave in the evening I would kiss him and then just hold him awhile. Since he always had a low-grade fever, I would tell him how nice and warm he felt to me. My hands always seem cold, and Scott would tell me they felt good on his warm body.

Most of my friends with AIDS react the same way. For example, when I held a PWA named Chad and hugged him, I told him he felt so nice and warm, just like Scott had felt to me when I had hugged him. I apologized for my cold hands, but Chad said that felt good to him. I told him his warm body reminded me of Scott. Chad smiled a big smile, and we didn't have to say anymore.

Finally, fear—especially the fear of dying—is always lurking in the background for PWAs. Sometimes, this fear can be a vehicle for finding the kind of love relationship with God that casts out fear.

When I first met Josie in 1992, she was an outspoken atheist. At that point she was HIV-positive but still fairly healthy. By 1995, she was in late-stage AIDS. At a workshop for PWAs, she described her increasing fear of death and her search to know if there really is a hereafter. During one time of prayer, she actually reached out publicly and addressed God by name. Without doubt, Josie's journey with HIV has opened up whole new spiritual vistas she might never have seen had it not been for this disease.

AIDS Lesson 13:

As the HIV disease progresses, PWAs (and their caregivers) often find that emotional and spiritual issues become more urgent. The resolution of emotional issues such as humiliation, anger, loneliness, guilt, and fear lies in the realm of the spiritual, where faith in God through Christ initiates a transformation that permeates one's whole being from the inside out.

Suggestions for PWAs

1. Your doctors can and want to help you in your fight against AIDS, and you should become as informed as you possibly can about what to expect. It is easier to face crises if you are prepared, so study, listen, and ask a lot of questions.
2. If you are despised and rejected by some, you have a choice to make. You can adopt a victim mentality and become bitter, wasting a lot of your energy. Or you can do what Jesus did when He was about to be crucified. He prayed, "Father, forgive them. They don't know what they are doing." Through that simple prayer, He turned victimization into victory. You can do the same.
3. Expect your emotional and spiritual battles to be perhaps more intense than your physical ones. By adopting the perspective of faith in relation to humiliation, anger, guilt, loneliness, and fear, you can turn them into humility, power, forgiveness, solitude, and serenity.

Suggestions for Caregivers

1. Get into a support group where you can compare notes with others who are making this same journey, in the process transforming some of the potentially devastating surprises ahead into expectations you can handle.

2. One of these surprises is how much you will share with your PWA the feelings of being an outcast in a supposedly enlightened society. You may be outraged, and rightfully so, but if you really want to bring change to our society and not just retribution to a segment of it, the testimony of your faithfulness in adversity will be your best platform.

3. Realize that your PWA's experiences with humiliation, anger, guilt, loneliness, and fear will touch your very soul in perhaps some very uncomfortable ways. But if you persist, not only will you have the opportunity to help your PWA resolve these issues, but you will grow as well.

Should I Tell People I Am HIV-positive?

 **6**

Frank and Jenny, both highly educated professionals, adopted Billie when he was two years old. Soon after, Billie was tested for HIV due to some underlying medical problems. Billie's test returned HIV-positive.

Although Frank and Jenny are not concerned about the HIV being spread to their other child, also adopted, letting other people know about this has been, with few exceptions, one long nightmare. Even their extended family has not handled it well.

They explained, "They said they would be there for us. But they're not. And I don't mean just the adults. The other children, if Billie as much as touches them, will jump back and shout, 'Get him off me. He's got AIDS. I'm gonna get AIDS.' They just really freak out.

"I don't want any of *them* coming to Billie's funeral. I don't *want* them coming to his deathbed. I don't want them around."

Billie is still feeling well. He has no symptoms of AIDS at this point. But now that he's old enough to have friends, sometimes Billie gets invited to spend the day with one or more of them, which poses a huge dilemma for Frank and Jenny. They know that most parents would want to know if an HIV-infected child were coming to play. They also know that most parents, knowing this, would not welcome such a visit. Should they let Billie go but not reveal his status? Or if not, will it all come back on them from the other parents once Billie gets sick?

Frank and Jenny live in fear. They have tried to find a church and have settled on one in the metropolitan area where a friend attends.

Over the telephone they told me, "We are really low. We're just really down. Can you find us a support group in our part of the country?"

David and Claire's experience has been similar. They adopted Sarah from an orphanage in Russia several years ago. After they brought Sarah home and the adoption was finalized, this young couple discovered that their daughter was HIV-positive. They chose to love her even more, but they needed support.

When they moved to the Portland area they wanted to find a church where they could worship and belong. So they visited a large evangelical church which they liked very much. They wanted to become part of that church family, so David called the church, thinking that the direct approach would be best. He asked to speak to one of the pastors.

"We're new in the area," David explained, "and we like your church."

"Good," the pastor said. "We're glad to have you."

"But there is one thing you should know," David continued. "A couple of years ago, we adopted a little Russian girl. Recently we learned that she is HIV-positive.

Are you prepared to have a family like ours worship with you?"

On the other end, there was a long pause. Evidently this was not a question the pastor had heard very often, if ever.

Finally, the reply came, "I'm sorry, but I don't think we are ready for you. Perhaps it would be better if you go elsewhere."

As you can imagine, David, who had summoned up all his courage in order to make this call in the first place, felt hurt by this and utterly rejected, not only for himself and his family, but especially for Sarah, who had visited the church with them and attended her age-group's Sunday school class and children's church. David didn't mention that part. Obviously, this church wanted to keep pretending that AIDS was not their problem, and that no HIV-positive people had ever or would ever bring this disease to their safe cloister.

He hung up, sadly. As a result, he kept his family home on Sundays for the next year. When you have been wounded like that, you are scared. You don't want the arrows to hit you again, so you retreat to a safe place. For many PWAs and their families, home seems like the only safe place, which is why many of them keep their secret "in the closet."

After awhile, however, David and Claire did some research and found a church with a more reasonable, responsible perspective. They are now a part of that church, where everyone knows about Sarah's situation.

The church has an HIV policy, and their nursery workers and Sunday school teachers have been educated about HIV disease. Sarah and her family are not excluded in any way from church activities. Instead, they feel accepted, appreciated, supported—in a word, they feel loved, which is what the church is supposed to be about.

AIDS Lesson 14:

Very few people are prepared to hear that an HIV-positive person has become part of their social circle (family, church, school, club, etc.). The choice for PWAs and their caregivers is between anger and bitterness and searching harder for a more reasonable, enlightened group.

In reality, there is no globally correct answer to this chapter's question. Telling others you have HIV is risky. But life is full of risks, and if we never take a risk, we're going to miss out on a lot of opportunities.

Personally speaking, I think the risk is worth taking, because the value of finding some support far outweighs the hurt of further rejection. If you are a PWA, you already know about rejection. A little more on top of what you already have experienced may not make much difference. But think of the difference that finding some support would make! How refreshing to find a group with whom you can be who you are, no facades, no games . . . just you.

We could have hidden Scott in Los Angeles. We could have chosen that his medical care occur there. Scott himself was torn between coming home to Oak Harbor and staying with Charly. But had he stayed there we might be living a lie to this day. Like some parents of PWAs who have died, we might have said, "Scott died of cancer (or pneumonia, or whatever)." Just knowing that this would be only a half-truth would gnaw at me constantly.

For us, openness and honesty was and still is the best approach. We can say, without diminishing our respect for Scott or dimming his memory in the slightest bit, "Our son, Scott, whom we loved dearly and miss desperately, died of AIDS."

I realize that not all parents are comfortable handling it this way. For example, I recall how my good friend, Trent, whose rather affluent parents live in Florida, came to Washington state with end-stage AIDS. Trent's parents knew that he had AIDS; however, they never even told anyone that Trent was sick, much less that he had AIDS.

As Trent was dying at one of the large hospitals in Seattle, his parents came to visit. Although it was very obvious to everyone else—the medical staff, Trent's partner, Eli, and possibly even to Trent—that Trent was dying, his parents came in one day, and the next day announced that they would be leaving because there wasn't anything they could do for him.

Eli took them out into the hall and got right into their face, and said, "Can't you see that Trent is dying? Don't leave him now."

They stayed until Trent died, then left immediately to go home. As Eli put them on the airplane, the mother said, "Thank you, Eli, for doing my job for me. You were the mother that I should have been when Trent needed me."

Trent's body was flown to Florida, where a memorial service was held. Never was it known or did they admit that Trent had died of AIDS. Rather, everyone thought he had died of cancer.

I often wonder what goes through those parents' minds when they hear about AIDS every day on the news, a disease that invaded their lives and ruined their dreams. Do they still deny it, or have they found a group of friends with whom they can be open and real?

As far as I'm concerned, this is the only route to recovery. But it isn't easy. Meg's husband, Steve, was in the final throes of AIDS. One afternoon, Meg and I had a long conversation over a cup of tea. She looked right at me and said with sincerity that would be shocking if I didn't know how difficult it is to tell the truth about AIDS, "You know, Mignon, Steve isn't dying of AIDS. He's dying of cancer."

As she said this, I thought, *It's easier for Meg to say Steve is dying of cancer than to say he's dying of AIDS.*

Because of her fear of other people's reactions, Meg was groping for a way of escape. It made me sad, and it still does every time I encounter this kind of denial, to think that people like Meg, already burdened beyond human endurance and longing for love, feel compelled through the fear of others to live a lie, the guilt of which will only add to their burden in the long run.

I think of one couple, both of whom have AIDS. She got it through tainted blood in 1983. He got it from her. Despite the fact that they acquired AIDS "the good way," these dear people live in total fear that others will come to know their secret, and that they will be evicted from their apartment, which is all they have, now that neither of them can work.

Social services told me that this couple could use my help. Yet even when I called and introduced myself as a person who had lost a son to AIDS, it still took them a long time to trust me. As I came to know them, I realized that the wife was wasting very rapidly, partly because she didn't have the energy to prepare any food.

She told me that they used to have a microwave, but now they didn't because when they had moved from another state, a volunteer agency required them to return the used one they had been loaned. I went out and got them a microwave and bought some groceries. When Bob and I brought these to them, they said, "You mean this is for us? Is it ours?"

"Yes, it's yours," we said.

"You mean it's ours to keep?"

"Yours to keep. It's a gift from our organization, *Support for the Journey*."

Then I discovered that the husband was running a temperature, but they didn't have a thermometer. So we went to the drugstore and got them a thermometer.

Next he told us that he hadn't been able to sit for days because of a hemorrhoid flare-up, so we went back to the drugstore and got some over-the-counter medications for that.

In that one day, I wrote five checks for them. The woman was moved to tears. "Promise me you'll come back," she begged. "Promise you won't forget us."

"We won't forget you," I promised. "We'll come back."

This story is crucial for two reasons: First, because what has happened to this couple is happening to other people all over our country (and our world) right now. Their health and their future have been shattered by HIV, and instead of experiencing compassionate care from society, they live in abject fear that everything else they need in order to survive will be ripped away from them too if people find out. Second, it is crucial because it shows how lonely and nearly impossible AIDS can be if you don't have some kind of support. I am confident that they would be far better off if they could connect with the kind of friends that the members of our support group could be for them, but when people are terrified to take the risk, there is no way short of violating their rights to force them to reach out for help.

AIDS Lesson 15:

Telling the truth about AIDS is always better than denial, pretending, or outright lying. Some people may reject you, but only if people know the truth can they truly help you resolve the pain.

I'd like to close this chapter with two stories that show what can happen when PWAs take the risk and others respond positively. I've already told you a little about Josh (chapter 2), but I didn't mention the way his family found out he had AIDS.

Josh had been living out in the woods in a trailer by himself. Although he struggled with homosexuality, he rarely "acted out," but as a result he acquired HIV. His health was failing, but no one knew it until he returned home to attend his aunt's funeral. His mother took one look at him and said, "Josh, you cannot go back into the woods until you go to the doctor. You look just awful."

Josh went to the doctor the following day. He had a bad case of Pneumocystis carinii pneumonia, a diagnosis for AIDS. Had he not been home at that particular time, he probably would have died out in the woods, alone.

Josh told his brothers and sisters that he had AIDS, but he couldn't bear to tell his parents. So he told them he had a rare form of pneumonia.

His mother thought Pneumocystis carinii pneumonia was really quite a term, and it took her a few tries to learn to pronounce it. So, in her Christmas letter she told all the relatives that this is what Josh had, not realizing that she was in effect telling everyone that Josh had AIDS.

One day about five months after that, when it was clear that Josh was not regaining his health totally, his dad came over to visit him at his sister's house. After they had talked for awhile, he asked, "Josh, have you ever considered the possibility that you might have HIV?"

Josh started to cry and he said, "Yes, Dad, I do have AIDS." And he said through his tears, "Now I suppose you want to know how I got it."

"No, no," his eighty-four-year-old father replied. "This is enough for one day. And anyway, everyone's entitled to one mistake."

Once his parents knew, Josh thought others should be told the truth. He kept saying to his mother, "Mom, you know if you told your friends and our relatives, they would be accepting, and it would be okay." But she was afraid, so Josh's secret stayed in the closet until several months before he died.

Now, looking back, she often says to me, "You know, Josh was right. Almost everyone responded lovingly."

Josh's funeral was a celebration of his life, during which it was known that he had died of AIDS.

Finally, the story of Jim and Laura illustrates what can happen when people have been properly educated about HIV, the needs of those infected and affected, and how Christian compassion requires us to respond.

In our area, a pastor named Bruce wanted to become involved in HIV/AIDS ministry. As a result, his church formulated an HIV policy.

Because this groundwork had been done, Jim and Laura, a young couple who had been married in the church and were quite active in it, called this pastor because Jim was very sick and in the hospital with CMV. The doctors had suggested he be tested for HIV. Their worst fears were confirmed. Jim had AIDS.

Here they were, their whole lives before them, and suddenly all those dreams seemed shattered.

The pastor counseled them, and after everything was in place, they told their families, their friends, and their church family. Because they were open and honest they have been surrounded with love and compassion.

AIDS Lesson 16:

Through proper education and preparation, people can be led to respond constructively to PWAs and their caregivers. This transforms a tragedy that could be made worse by judgmental attitudes into one with diminished impact because it was shared, for "a sorrow shared is a sorrow diminished."

Suggestions for PWAs

1. Expect to experience extreme tension between needing to tell people you have HIV and anxiety about how they will react. Both the need and the anxiety are legitimate.

2. When you sense rejection because someone has learned you are HIV-positive, try to avoid anger or bitterness, since these will be destructive to you. Ignorance breeds fear. You can try to educate them, but keep in mind that they may not be ready yet to learn what you have to teach, so your input may only be the beginning of their own enlightenment.

3. Find a safe place where you can be yourself, a group to whom you can speak the whole truth and nothing but the truth about how you feel and who you are. Your first experience(s) with this may not be positive. But don't give up easily. You need this support, so keep looking until you find it.

4. As much as possible, do not allow anyone to lie about your disease. You deserve the opportunity to live and die as authentically as possible.

Suggestions for Caregivers

1. Realize that it will seem easier to hide "in the closet" than to risk facing negatives from others in relation to you or your PWA. After all, you have your hands full with the disease itself. The problem is that sometime in the journey you will need others, and then you may have less energy to communicate with them than you do now.

2. As much as you can, funnel educational materials about HIV/AIDS to people in your social circle, especially those you may need as the disease progresses. The more they know, the more likely they will be to help you.

3. Plug yourself and your PWA into some kind of support network—possibly even different groups—where you can listen and learn from others, and they from you. You will gain insight and strength for your journey simply by being with your fellow pilgrims and seeing that it is indeed possible to survive this ordeal.

4. Refuse to lie about your PWA's disease, while always respecting that person's right to privacy if he or she is not ready for others to know.

Mom/Dad, May I Come Home?

7 In August 1988, after Scott almost died of CMV complications, he faced a crisis. He was too weak and sick to take care of himself any longer. But after recovering from this bout, he would soon be released from the Century City Hospital.

Where could he go? Who would take care of him? The natural answers for Scott, as for most PWAs when they face these questions, were *home* and *family*.

Home, where the roses would be blooming and he could sleep in his own room and watch TV and listen to music or just think in our quiet family room. And family— his mom and dad could take care of him. He knew this in his heart, but he wondered: *After all I've put them through during the past few years, would they want me home?*

When I came into his hospital room one morning, Scott began to cry. "Mom," he asked, "may I come home?"

"Yes, Scott," I replied immediately. "Dad and I would love to have you come home."

"Mom, I don't mean for a visit. I mean to *stay*."

"I know, Scott. We would love to have you come home."

Just to be sure, he asked me again. Scott needed to hear it repeated because we had experienced such difficult times together earlier when he was using alcohol and drugs.

"What will the people in Oak Harbor think?" he asked. "I would be the first person to come home to live and die with AIDS."

"You'll be safe and protected at home with Dad and me," I said. "But I can't answer for anyone else."

"Mom, what about Charly?" he asked.

"He and I have discussed this already, Scott," I said. "Charly doesn't think he could care for you and keep up his work at the accounting firm."

When Charly came to the hospital after work that day, and the three of us were alone in Scott's room, Scott asked Charly to close the door. Then he said, "Charly, I have decided to go home with my mom."

They both began to cry. Scott explained what we all knew, "I can no longer take care of myself. My mom isn't working and she can take care of me."

Tears rolled down my cheeks as I listened to these two young men who loved each other, as they grappled with a dreaded disease that was bigger than both of them. They had lived so carelessly at times—partying, drinking, doing drugs, living on the edge. Life had been so exciting, but so dangerous! Now they were facing the consequences, and they needed help . . . our help. And God's help.

Scott's next task was to call his dad, which wasn't necessary as far as I was concerned. But Scott insisted on doing it. "Dad, may I come home?" were the only words Scott got out before he began to cry again.

"Sure, Scott," Bob replied immediately. Scott loved his dad so much, and Bob loved Scott more than words can express. There had been some rough years, but now all of that seemed to vanish.

"Dad, who will take care of me?" Scott was referring to a physician. The doctors at Century City Hospital had told Scott we had to get his medical team in place before they would release him. Scott needed to have a local physician as well as an infectious disease specialist who would agree to care for Scott.

"Who would you like me to ask?" Bob asked.

"Dr. Teays," Scott replied. Dr. Teays had been our family doctor for many years, and he was very active in the church that Scott would probably attend. "Do you think he would do it?"

"I'll ask him," Bob replied. "I'll call you back."

That night Bob called and described his meeting with Dr. Teays. "Scott has AIDS," Bob had explained. "And he's been very sick in Century City Hospital. Now he has asked to come home. We are so happy about this decision and want to do our best for Scott. He needs to have a primary care physician here and asked if you would be willing to help in that way."

"Yes, Bob," Dr. Teays said, tears welling up in his eyes. "Of course. It would be a privilege." Then he gave Bob a big hug and they wept together.

A few days later—August 31, 1988—Scott and I traveled home together. After all we'd been through in the past few weeks, we both needed to return to where our family began. Charly brought Scott some street clothes to wear home. They were so big on Scott. It forced me to realize how much weight Scott had lost.

"You look great, Scott," we both told him, which was true, comparatively speaking. One thing that really looked incomparably great was the big smile on Scott's face, a smile that only changed for a little while when it came time to say good-bye to Charly. Scott expected he would never see him again.

When we got to Oak Harbor, Scott's sister Wendy and Bob had everything in place. The house was spotless, ready for our arrival. The lawn and garden were groomed, and the roses were blooming profusely. Scott checked it all. He was delighted to be home, a delight we all shared.

Two of our friends brought dinner that evening, and it tasted so good! I was amazed when they brought their children with them and even had them shake Scott's hand. What a welcome home. They weren't afraid to touch Scott. Inwardly, I thanked God!

Later that evening other family members came to see Scott. It all went very well. If there were any fears of HIV, they were well hidden. "Welcome home, Scott," was what everyone said, each in his or her own way.

When I finally laid my head on my pillow that night, it was with a sense of gratitude that we had made this transition so smoothly. While we didn't know where the journey with AIDS would take us or how long that journey would take, we did know that our son, whose life for the past few years had caused us such concern, had finally come back to us.

At that moment, we could identify with the father of the prodigal son that Jesus told about in the New Testament (Luke 15:11–32). That man's son had taken his inheritance and squandered it on loose living. But for that son, as for ours, the loss of everything helped him come to his senses, as a result of which he returned home, repentant and humble, willing to become like one of his father's hired hands.

The father, who had obviously been watching and waiting, did not make him bow and scrape, but welcomed him back with open arms. "When he was still a great way off," Jesus said, "his father saw him and had compassion, and ran and fell on his neck and kissed him" (v. 20). Then the father threw a big party in the son's honor, despite the angry protest of another son who had stayed home and played it straight while his brother was out on the town.

"It was right that we should make merry and be glad," the father explained, "for your brother was dead and is alive again, and was lost and is found" (v. 32).

Jesus told this parable to the self-righteous religious leaders of His day to describe how the love of the Father, God, operates when a repentant wanderer returns home. Human beings may tend to judge PWAs who want to come home, but God's concerns are forgiveness, restoration, and a renewal of relationships. That's what we wanted with Scott, and even though it took AIDS to bring him full circle, we welcomed the result.

AIDS Lesson 17:

At some point in their journey with AIDS, most PWAs will want to return home, either to be reconciled or to die, or both. The families who most constructively process this are those who prepare for it.

Before I suggest how to make this decision, let's think briefly about the real meaning of the question itself: "Mom/Dad, may I come home?" When PWAs ask this, they're not asking only for a physical place to be, although that is part of it. They're also asking to come back into their parents' lives, to reclaim that special place in their parents' hearts that is reserved for them. Parents usually know its implications, at least intuitively.

Some parents will welcome this, as we did. When this happens, it presents the whole family with an opportunity for healing and restoration. That's what happened for Bart, who spent his final two weeks at home. Bart's five brothers and sisters, together with their parents, provided his care around the clock as he slowly wasted away. They bathed him, turned him, gave him his medications, all of which brought closure to his life because it restored his place in the family.

Not only that, the experience, difficult as it was, gave his family a wonderful opportunity to love him as no one else could. The net result for all of them was a special bond that only comes from having participated together in a truly significant experience.

Other families, for one reason or another, are not as open to having a PWA return home. After weeks of contemplation and prayer, Luke decided to tell his family about his diagnosis. Over the telephone he said, "Mom and Dad, I have AIDS." For them this news was horrifying and their suspicions about Luke's lifestyle were confirmed.

The parents were in shock, angry and confused. The words they exchanged were not loving. They all needed time to process what had happened. They thought Luke would be dying very soon, and they were afraid of the HIV.

"Luke, we love you," they said. "But you can't come home. We don't want to get HIV from you. We don't want anyone to know you are homosexual either. You will just have to stay where you are and find help there."

Luke was devastated. *My family doesn't want me! They are afraid of me! I am alone and I'm going to get sick and die!* were his thoughts. The sickness and the dying he could deal with, but the rejection from his family was unbearable.

Over time, Luke came to a peace about his relationship with his family, with whom I've talked by phone. They are still definite about how they feel toward this disease and

how Luke became infected. I can't change their hearts—
only God can do that—but I can keep in touch with them,
encourage them, and love them.

Sometimes parents would like to care for a PWA, but
they realize that they simply don't have the physical, emotional, or spiritual resources to do so. For Joyce, her
reluctance to have her son Randy come home when he
could no longer take care of himself was due to her lack of
space, for she knew based on what she had heard from
others that when a PWA comes home to die, part of the
house becomes a hospital room.

"He's been talking about coming home and asking us
about it," Joyce told me one night. "But we can't have him
in our home, not because we don't want to, but because
there is no place to put him."

I reassured her later. "There are group homes where
Randy can go when he needs that level of care," I said. "You
can visit Randy there as often as you want and you'll be able
to nurture him in that way. In fact, this might leave you
more energy to nurture him than if you had to turn him or
feed him, or change his diapers or do the laundry. It may
work out better for both of you."

For Molly, Frank's mom, the issue was that she didn't
have the time, energy, or strength that she knew Frank's
care would require. When Frank was in a hospice in the
final stages of AIDS, he kept asking to go home. He talked
about it all the time to anyone who would listen—doctors,
social workers, visitors, and most of all his parents.

Molly was torn. She and her husband had provided
care for Frank right up until his admission to the hospice.
Toward the end of that period, Molly told me, Frank's care
had become unmanageable for them. Due to his
neuropathy, he could no longer walk. A bout with diarrhea
meant that his sheets had to be changed three times a night.

Molly, working a full-time job and struggling with rheumatoid arthritis, had reached a point of utter exhaustion. After Frank entered the hospice, Molly spent at least one night a week in Frank's room, using the couch for a bed. She said it was her "night out," but he never knew that when she was there she slept poorly.

"What should I do, Mignon?" she asked me. "I don't think we can handle Frank at home. This, and his constant begging, makes me feel guilty, which just makes everything harder."

"I know exactly how you feel," I told her. "When Scott was hospitalized near the end, for the last three months, day after day, we and everybody else heard, 'I just want to go home.'"

The social workers had asked me if we could handle this. "Please don't put this on me," I told them. "It's too hard for me."

I was torn, exhausted, and I knew that bringing Scott home in his condition would strip away the last little bit of space I so desperately needed. If he came home, even with twenty-four-hour professional nursing care, there would be no privacy, nor would there be even a few minutes a day when I would be away from his dying. Of course it was always on my mind, but I was surviving by relishing little things like the picturesque twenty-minute ride to the hospital and back each day.

I also knew myself, that if I made the decision to keep him hospitalized I would always regret it, chastising myself that I had neglected him at the end, which wasn't true. But when you're in that situation, the issues that really nail you are not primarily intellectual, but emotional.

Ultimately the decision to keep Scott in the hospital was made by Scott's insurance company, which had been calling every day to see if he still met the criteria based on the computation that twenty-four-hour care at home would ultimately cost more than the $400 per day currently being paid for Scott's hospitalization. This worked out better for both of us, because it gave me the opportunity to regroup between trips to the hospital, which enabled me to be more helpful to Scott when I was with him.

AIDS Lesson 18:

The issue of home care is so complex, with its relational, emotional, and spiritual components, that help from others may be necessary in order to resolve it to everyone's satisfaction.

Suggestions for PWAs

1. Try to discern where your longing to return home is coming from. If it is being driven by your need to finish unfinished business, realize that your family may need some time before they feel the same way.

2. Recognize and try to accept that the "home" you left is not really the home to which you would return since all the individuals have changed over time.

3. If these changes resulted from your parents' grappling with your behavior, it would be wise to read the parable of the prodigal son and follow his example.

4. Recognize that your request will place tremendous pressure on your parents, especially your mother, who will probably care for you. In order to set everyone free to choose, you could say, "Of course you don't *have* to do this. But if you choose to, I will certainly appreciate your help, because I need it."

Suggestions for Caregivers

With my coauthor's help, I've developed the following checklist of issues to consider in the process of making this decision.

Gather your information first.

☐ I understand the level of physical care that will be required, and in conjunction with other helpers I am both willing and able to provide it. These helpers are: _____

☐ We have the financial resources we will need.

☐ We have the space necessary.

☐ I understand that bringing this person home means giving up my privacy until the journey is over.

☐ I have consulted the following sources for advice:

☐ the doctor(s), who said: _____

☐ social and case workers, who said: _____

☐ the insurance company, which said: _____

☐ our family, which said: _____

☐ our clergyperson, who said: _____

☐ my support group, which said: _____

☐ The consensus, if any, was:

☐ This decision should be made by the following date:

_____.

Consider the relational issues:

☐ I believe that bringing this person home might positively impact the following relationships: _____

☐ I believe that bringing this person home might negatively impact the following relationships: _____

☐ My spouse (if applicable) would prefer:

☐ I am not concerned/somewhat concerned/very concerned with what others may think if I bring _____ home, especially:_____

☐ The best way to deal with this concern would be: _____

Consider the emotional issues:

☐ My basic feeling toward _____ is: _____

☐ Bringing him/her home would:

    ☐ improve this

    ☐ make this worse

☐ My primary emotional motivation for considering this request is:

_____

☐ Refusing this request may cause me guilt, remorse, or regrets later.

☐ It is ☐ easy ☐ difficult ☐ impossible for me to admit that I have emotional limits.

☐ I believe that granting this request would leave me with more/less emotional reserves to direct toward this person's best interests.

Consider the spiritual issues:

☐ I have a sense of anxiety/neutrality/peace when I think about _____'s spiritual condition, and I believe that bringing him/her home at this point would/would not impact this.

☐ I believe that in relation to this request, God wants me to: _____

Think creatively:

☐ I have considered alternatives to an all-or-nothing decision, such as short day trips in the area, or even short visits home.

☐ I have allowed myself the freedom to say no or yes to this request, without compulsion or coercion, and over the long term I will not allow anyone to heap guilt on me, because I made this decision in good faith, with a clear conscience before God.

My decision is: _____

But I Don't Want to Die

 **8** Most PWAs, sometime in their journey, will say: "I don't want to die." Often, this may be more an expression of deep sadness that life, which held such promise, is too soon nearing its end.

This was true of Gene. Gene wanted desperately to live. With the rugged good looks of Robert Redford, he had a thriving career in the computer field. He also had a unique sense of humor and a wonderful personality. Gene had so much to live for and conversely so much to lose.

He would say to me, "Mignon, if only I hadn't been so careless when I was with women," or "Mignon, why was I so foolish? I don't want to die yet. I'm too young to die."

Fred said the same thing in almost the same words. After college Fred had gone to work for a large corporation. He enjoyed his single life to the limit. Wine, women, and song filled Fred's single years.

He knew he was HIV-positive when he met Paige, a beautiful woman, who married him anyway. Shortly after their wedding Fred's health began to decline. He experienced awful night sweats, then low-grade fevers.

"Why did I do the things I did?" he asked. "I don't want to die! I have so much to live for! I don't want to leave my beautiful wife! Please God, don't let me die!" was his cry.

When I hear my friends talk like this, I always recall a particular conversation Scott and I had about ten months after he came home. I was rubbing his feet and legs. Scott was dwelling on the slow but steady decline in his health and strength. "Mom," he said, "I just wish I could gain some more strength. I don't have any energy."

"I know, Scott. I wish you could too," I said. "But we have a lot to be thankful for, you've lived beyond the nine months that the doctor gave us. Maybe you'll live another twenty-four months."

"But, Mom," he said, "that isn't a very long time."

"Maybe you'll live three years."

Again he said, "But, Mom, that's not a very long time. There's so much I wanted to do with my life. I'm not afraid to die, but I don't want to die."

This sentiment is perhaps captured best in poetry, of which one of Scott's favorites was:

Fern Hill
by Dylan Thomas

Now as I was young and easy under the apple boughs
About the lilting house and happy as the grass was green,
The night above the dingle starry,
Time let me hail and climb
Golden in the heydays of his eyes,
And honoured among wagons I was prince of the apple towns
And once below a time I lordly had the trees and leaves
Trail with daisies and barley
Down the rivers of the windfall light.

And as I was green and carefree, famous among the barns
About the happy yard and singing as the farm was home,
In the sun that is young once only,
Time let me play and be
Golden in the mercy of his means,
And green and golden I was huntsman and herdsman, the calves
Sang to my horn, the foxes on the hills barked clear and cold,
And the sabbath rang slowly in the pebbles of the holy streams.

All the sun long it was running, it was lovely, the hay
Fields high as the house, the tunes from the chimneys, it was air
And playing, lovely and watery
And fire green as grass.
And nightly under the simple stars
As I rode to sleep the owls were bearing the farm away,
All the moon long I heard, blessed among stables, the nightjars
Flying with the ricks, and the horses
Flashing into the dark.

And then to awake, and the farm, like a wanderer white
With the dew, come back, the cock on his shoulder; it was all
Shining, it was Adam and maiden,
The sky gathered again
And the sun grew round that very day.
So it must have been after the birth of the simple light
In the first, spinning place, the spellbound horses walking warm
Out of the whinnying green stable
On to the fields of praise.

And honoured among foxes and pheasants by the gay house
Under the new made clouds and happy as the heart was long,
In the sun born over and over,
I ran my heedless ways,
My wishes raced through the house-high hay

And nothing I cared, at my sky blue trades, that time allows
In all his tuneful turnings so few and such morning songs
Before the children green and golden
Follow him out of grace,

Nothing I cared, in the lamb white days, that time would take me
Up to the swallow thronged loft by the shadow of my hand,
In the moon that is always rising,
Nor that riding to sleep
I should hear him fly with the high fields
And wake to the farm forever fled from the childless land.
Oh as I was young and easy in the mercy of his means,
Time held me green and dying
Though I sang in my chains like the sea. [1]

AIDS Lesson 19:
Most PWAs will at some point struggle with intense sadness over dying prematurely. There is no point in trying to talk them out of this, because they must work through it to get beyond it.

As Scott's disease progressed, his sadness over dying young changed to anxiety in relation to death itself. About six weeks before Scott died, after Bob and I had been with him all day, the phone rang. It was Scott from the hospital.

"Mom," he said, "I'm afraid."

Nighttime was the hardest time for him, especially toward the end. I don't know if it was the darkness, or the fact that he would be alone overnight, or that he had more time to think about his approaching death, or all of these factors. As the disease progressed, Scott became more dependent on us. He wanted one of us with him much of the time.

"Do you want us to come back, Scott?" I asked, hoping he would say no. I had only been home long enough to take a hot bath and start to shift gears. But we were willing to go back if he really needed us.

"No," he replied. "I just need to talk."

Bob picked up the extension, and we talked. And we listened.

What we heard was like turning back the clock. You know, when the kids are little and it's dark in their room, and the conversation goes something like this:

"What are you worried about, Scotter?"

"I think there's a monster under my bed, Daddy."

"Really? Well, let's just have a look under there."

They get a flashlight and shine it into the darkness.

"I don't see anything, Scotter, do you?"

"No, Daddy. But I'm still afraid."

"Well, Mommy and Daddy are here."

"I know. But I'm still afraid."

"And Jesus is here too."

"I know, but I can't see Him."

"But we can pray. You pray with me. Now I lay me down to sleep, I pray the Lord my soul to keep. If I should die before I wake, I pray the Lord my soul to take."

"Thanks, Daddy. I think I can go to sleep now."

We realized, as we walked with Scott toward the inevitable conclusion of his journey with AIDS, that the primary questions he had were no longer physical or intellectual, but emotional and spiritual. He needed—we all needed—spiritual support.

The morning after this particular call, Bob was in Scott's hospital room when the doctors made their rounds.

Dr. Teays suggested this. "I think what you need is spiritual reinforcement," he said.

Scott agreed. "I think that I would like some men from my church to come and pray and study the Bible with me," he said.

"I think I know someone who might like to do this," Dr. Teays replied.

The very next day, retired Superior Court Judge Howard Patrick visited Scott for the first time. Judge Patrick, who was a family friend as well, came to read and pray with Scott every day for the rest of Scott's life. Scott was very comforted by this and often fell asleep listening to a devotional or prayer by this wonderful man who has since joined Scott in heaven. By the time Scott died, he was ready, and no longer afraid.

This same progression occurred for Gene and Fred. Before Gene developed late-stage AIDS, he had never attended church and wasn't interested in spiritual matters. But as he looked death in the eye, he began to wonder. *What happens after I die? Is there a hereafter?*

When he asked me those questions, I shared about my own faith journey and that I could never have faced AIDS and the accompanying issues had it not been for my faith.

"I would never have been able to say good-bye to Scott if I knew I would never see him again," I said. "How could I watch him die without hope of eternal life?"

"You make it sound like it's actually true, Mignon."

"It is, Gene. You just have to believe."

I gave him a New Testament and he began to read. He started in Romans, then read John. By the time he died, Gene was a true believer. He knew a real peace and was not afraid anymore.

For Fred, things went more slowly. As his disease progressed, he went on disability. Paige was a beautician and worked long hours, during which Fred was home alone. We would talk on the telephone often and I would visit him. He told me how lonely he was, and that the last few hours of the day before Paige came home he had to work and concentrate on getting his spirits up. Then when she arrived each evening they would talk and cry together.

I shared with him how Scott grieved the losses in his life, feeling depressed as well. "But Mignon," he said, "Scott had you with him all day long. I'm here all by myself."

Fred's nurse came to draw blood twice a week. Fred began sharing his real feelings with her, especially that he was beginning to think about God more and more. She asked him if he would like a visit from a Christian friend of hers. Fred was elated at the idea.

Jack visited Fred often. They talked about spiritual things, going only as far as Fred wanted to go each time. Soon Fred only wanted to talk about what it really meant to be a Christian. When he received Christ, Fred experienced God's forgiveness. As he focused on God and what it would be like living forever with Him, his depression decreased. When he died, he knew the "peace that passes all understanding."

AIDS Lesson 20:

For the PWA, the prospect of dying causes anxiety. This is true even for believers, but their experience can end in acceptance because faith promises a life beyond.

All of my friends who are living with AIDS know that I won't throw Scripture at them or preach to them. This is not my style. I believe God has called me to first of all love them right where they are. But when they ask me where my strength comes, I tell them that my Christian faith sustained me through Scott's illness and death, as it sustains me now. Without faith, I would have nothing of real substance to offer PWAs or their caregivers. Oh, I could love them and try to help them, but if this life is all there is, everything we do or try to do is ultimately an exercise in futility.

If, however, there is a God who put in us a soul that longs to know Him and then return to Him, then it is only sensible that PWAs (and their caregivers), who face more fully than most other human beings the prospect of death, should at least carefully examine the value of faith. One of the best ways to do this, besides getting close to an authentic believer, is to get out the Bible and search it for yourself. To facilitate this process, my coauthor and I have selected a few of the many key Scripture passages that could prove helpful to you. Our only suggestion, to both PWAs and their caregivers, is that you let these words penetrate all the way to your soul, for if you do, you will have found the key to eternal life, and the only real antidote to the ultimate human fear expressed in the words, "But I don't want to die."

For the caregiver who's PWA refuses to discuss faith issues, it is important to let go of these concerns, trusting God to bring His peace in His time. However, it is so important that you keep loving and providing support in physical and emotional areas. Remember, we are not God. He is able to do His perfect work with or without us.

Helpful Scriptures

When you are afraid . . .
Psalm 23
The LORD is my shepherd;
I shall not want.
He makes me to lie down in green pastures;
He leads me beside the still waters.
He restores my soul;
He leads me in the paths of righteousness
For His name's sake.

Yea, though I walk through the valley of the shadow of death,
I will fear no evil;
For You are with me;
Your rod and Your staff, they comfort me.

You prepare a table before me in the presence of my enemies;
You anoint my head with oil;
My cup runs over.
Surely goodness and mercy shall follow me
All the days of my life;
And I will dwell in the house of the LORD
Forever.

(See also Ps. 56:3–4; Isa. 12:2; 41:13; 43:2; 49:15; Matt. 11:28.)

When you need forgiveness . . .
Psalm 103:11-14
For as the heavens are high above the earth,
So great is His mercy toward those who fear Him;
As far as the east is from the west,
So far has He removed our transgressions from us.
As a father pities his children,

So the LORD pities those who fear Him.
For He knows our frame;
He remembers that we are dust.

(See also Ps. 86:5; 1 John 1:9.)

When you need a reminder of God's love . . .
John 3:16
For God so loved the world that He gave His only begotten Son,
that whoever believes in Him should not perish but have everlast-
ing life.

Romans 8:38–39
For I am persuaded that neither death nor life, nor angels nor
principalities nor powers, nor things present nor things to come,
nor height nor depth, nor any other created thing, shall be able
to separate us from the love of God which is in Christ Jesus our
Lord.

When you need assurance of everlasting life . . .
John 5:24
Most assuredly, I say to you, he who hears My word and believes
in Him who sent Me has everlasting life, and shall not come into
judgment, but has passed from death into life.

John 11:25–26
Jesus said to her, "I am the resurrection and the life. He who
believes in Me, though he may die, he shall live. And whoever lives
and believes in Me shall never die. Do you believe this?"

(See also John 10:28.)

When you need hope . . .
Romans 5:1–5
Therefore, having been justified by faith, we have peace with God
through our Lord Jesus Christ, through whom also we have access

by faith into this grace in which we stand, and rejoice in hope of the glory of God. And not only that, but we also glory in tribulations, knowing that tribulation produces perseverance; and perseverance, character; and character, hope. Now hope does not disappoint, because the love of God has been poured out in our hearts by the Holy Spirit who was given to us.

When you need peace . . .

John 14:27

Peace I leave with you, My peace I give to you; not as the world gives do I give to you. Let not your heart be troubled, neither let it be afraid.

John 16:33

These things I have spoken to you, that in Me you may have peace. In the world you will have tribulation; but be of good cheer, I have overcome the world.

Philippians 4:6-7

Be anxious for nothing, but in everything by prayer and supplication, with thanksgiving, let your requests be made known to God; and the peace of God, which surpasses all understanding, will guard your hearts and minds through Christ Jesus.

When you wonder where everything is headed . . .

1 Corinthians 15:53–54

For this corruptible must put on incorruption, and this mortal must put on immortality. So when this corruptible has put on incorruption, and this mortal has put on immortality, then shall be brought to pass the saying that is written: "Death is swallowed up in victory."

Revelation 21:4

And God will wipe away every tear from their eyes; there shall be no more death, nor sorrow, nor crying. There shall be no more pain, for the former things have passed away.

PART
2

Issues Often Faced by Caregivers

How Can I Face This?

9 Scott survived his initial bout with CMV and actually regained some of his strength, but oh so briefly. There were nine hospitalizations during the next eight months, some lasting weeks at a time.

We were on a constant roller coaster—up and down, up and down. By the spring of 1989, he was beginning the decline he never climbed out of. On May 14, Mother's Day, we had a terrifying experience: Scott had his first seizure.

We were down in the family room—Scott, Wendy and Steve (Wendy's fiancé), Bob and me. I had just received some beautiful cards and gifts. Scott gave me four rosebushes to add to my rose garden. He and Bob had shopped for them the day before. We had hugs and kisses, then most of us went upstairs. Scott and Steve stayed put to watch television. I went to the kitchen to clean up our breakfast dishes. I had a habit of always glancing down into the family room from the kitchen to check on Scott. This time when I glanced down, Scott was well into a grand mal seizure.*

I was frightened and called for Bob. Since we had no experience with seizures and didn't know what to do, we dialed 911. Scott was taken to the hospital and returned home the next day. Dilantin* was prescribed to control the seizures, and blood draws* were taken to measure the Dilantin levels.

I asked the doctor what we should do if Scott had another seizure. I wanted to have my bases covered since Scott and I were alone much of the time. I just wanted to do my best for him.

Based on the doctor's advice, I assembled a little seizure kit* in a plastic bag, including gloves and tongue depressors with gauze taped around them. The doctor told me that the first thing to do in case of a seizure was to turn his head to the side so he wouldn't swallow his tongue, then insert the wrapped tongue depressors between his teeth so he wouldn't chew his tongue.

I also called several of our neighbors. "Scott's beginning to have seizures now," I said, "and I just want to know if I ever found myself really stuck, could I call you?" One neighbor, a retired physician, agreed to be "on call" if needed, as did some of our other neighbors.

It was a good thing I prepared myself. On Saturday morning, May 20, Bob had gone to have breakfast with the guys as he usually does on weekends. At 7:30, I was having my coffee downstairs in the family room when I heard Scott go to the kitchen one flight above and say, "Good morning." I knew he was going to take his morning pills with a bit of yogurt.

All of a sudden I heard those terrible guttural sounds. He hit the counter while a stool cracked against the cupboard. By the time I reached Scott, he was on the floor in the midst of a grand mal seizure—his hands contracted, his eyes rolled back, and his body went completely rigid with his head thrown back.

I grabbed my little seizure kit, turned his head to the side, and got the tongue depressor in his mouth. As he chewed on that, writhing on the floor, I grabbed the phone and dialed our doctor-neighbor, totally unaware of the time of day. All I knew was that I didn't really want to be alone with this. Thank God, help came.

AIDS Lesson 21:
The best way to face AIDS is together. Otherwise, it will eat you alive.

I was to learn that the physical aspects of AIDS would challenge me in many ways. On June 5, Scott traveled to Seattle with Father Tench. Scott's task was to participate for the Episcopal church in a panel discussion on AIDS.

I spent the day praying about two things: First, that Scott would find the right words to say. Second, and just as important, that the nausea that Scott had been struggling with wouldn't give Father Tench more to remember than he might care to.

Both prayers were answered. Scott never felt sick to his stomach that day. And, after the program, one of the other priests told Father Tench, "I feel the young man that came with you was truly a Christian."

Scott came home talking excitedly about the day—the panel, the people who attended, the setting, on and on. He was far more animated than he had been for months. As he shared, I asked if he was hungry.

"Not really," he said. "But I'd try a little spaghetti."

Spaghetti. His favorite meal, ever since he was little. I always had individual portions prepared in the freezer.

The meal hit the spot. But not long after supper, Scott went upstairs to the bathroom. "I think I'm getting sick," he said.

It was a false alarm. So back down he came, slowly, suffering from pain in his feet and legs.

I got out the basin and set it next to the couch along with paper towels and gloves for me, just in case.

Over the next few minutes he was up and down the stairs a couple of times. Then, just when he was convinced he wasn't going to throw up, he turned around from the toilet and projected spaghetti all over the bathroom and himself.

I heard him and ran upstairs to help. I could hardly believe my eyes.

Scott was distraught. "Oh, Mom, I'm sorry," he said.

"It's okay, Scott, it's okay," I replied. "Let's just get you cleaned up."

After we were back downstairs where he was comfortable and feeling okay, I said, "Now don't worry. I'm just going to go clean up that bathroom. It's okay."

It took me two hours.

As I worked, the realities of the past few weeks crowded my mind. Scott was downstairs, sick. There were indications that he was getting sicker. Bob was at a meeting. I was getting weary. We'd already traveled this way almost a year, but only God knew how far we had yet to go.

I was on my hands and knees in front of the bathtub, cleaning. I felt trapped, locked in. And at that moment I remember thinking, word for word, "Mignon, don't ever forget this night, because someone is always going to be feeling exactly like you feel right now." I always wrote down any unusual events on my calendar, along with the doctor appointments, blood draws, etc. I did not do this as journaling, but rather to keep appointments and an accurate log for doctor information. At that time writing a book to give others hope and encouragement wasn't even a thought for me. I just needed to get through our own journey one day at a time.

AIDS Lesson 22:
You will often feel trapped by AIDS. One way out is to remember that someone else will need help from one who understands what goes on behind closed doors when AIDS comes home.

Suggestions for Caregivers

1. Be honest and be open with your feelings about having to become an Emergency Medical Technician. If discussing these with your PWA is too hard, find someone in whom you can confide: This is *awful!* Worse that anything I ever imagined.

2. Line up help, as I did, but don't expect everyone to be willing or able to be "on call." Be thankful for those who are willing. Be forgiving of those who aren't.

3. Expect the unexpected. Then you'll be less often surprised by the twists and turns of AIDS. While it's true that the disease progression is somewhat unpredictable, trying to know for sure what will happen next in your individual case will be like nailing Jell-O to the wall.

4. How can you face this? You can't ... by yourself. Don't even try. Find a friend, even if the only one you can think of is God. After all, He has promised that you will never have to face more than you can bear.

5. Keep a journal. As you write, imagine someone like yourself whom you will someday meet. What do you long for? What do you need? If you keep track of these things, I am confident that after you have faced this, you will be able to help other caregivers face what they have to face.

Suggestions for PWAs

1. AIDS may force you to become more dependent on your caregiver than you might wish to be. It is better to face the frustration or embarrassment head on than to pretend it doesn't bother you.
2. Give your caregiver an opportunity to describe his or her feelings about this too. Don't be surprised, hurt, or offended if you hear words of fear or revulsion. These are not directed toward you but toward what is happening to you. The deeper the hurt, the more you know you are loved.
3. Direct the negative emotions toward the disease while using positive emotions (such as thankfulness that someone cares enough *about* you to care *for* you) to build your strength and your relationships.
4. How can you face this? You can't . . . by yourself. But true strength in the face of adversity comes through admitting that we are weak.

What to Say When You Don't Know What to Say

10 Before our journey with AIDS introduced us to a world we knew nothing about and immersed us in issues that threatened to overwhelm us, I thought I knew the answers to a lot more questions than I do today.

Now that I've walked this pathway with scores of people, however, I have to admit that sometimes I have more questions than I do answers, because as my coauthor says, "Every good question leads to a better question." In other words, sometimes the best answer to a question is another question because it keeps the inquirer talking, and in the process he or she may discover some new insight or perspective on his or her own problem.

Many times during Scott's long journey, he made statements or asked questions that made me painfully aware that I simply didn't know what to say. For example, Scott had just been home ten days when he was having some breathing problems. He had a temperature and pain in his chest as well. The home-health nurse came to check on him, and she and the doctor decided that Scott needed to be admitted to the hospital.

Scott was lying down on the backseat of the car as Bob and I drove him to the hospital. Slowly he sat up, looked out, and gazed at the beautiful water that surrounds the island and the mountains in the distance. He started to cry. He said, "Why is all this happening so fast? I don't want to go yet." He thought he was getting Pneumocystis carinii pneumonia again, and knowing he almost died the first time, he was frightened.

We rode in silence. Neither Bob nor I knew what to say. We were afraid to say anything. My eyes welled up with tears. I tilted my head upward so the tears wouldn't spill down my cheeks. I had to be brave for Scott. I prayed, "Lord, give us all the strength to face this journey. God, only You can help us blaze these trails, one at a time."

Why is all this happening so fast? What can you say to that kind of question? When we arrived at the hospital I was still speechless. All I could do was shake my head and hold back my tears as I rubbed Scott's legs and back. Then I sat silently in the room with him while he slept. Scott really appreciated falling asleep and waking up knowing I was there, even if I couldn't change anything about what was happening.

For a long time I was uncomfortable with the idea that just being there was the best I could do, because I am both activistic and talkative by nature. When there is a problem, I want to fix it, offer some advice about how it might be fixed, or both. With AIDS, however, I was thrust into a setting where silence is usually better than most of the words people offer, since no advice, wise as it may seem, will really be helpful . . . unless the PWA asks for it.

Remember the classic case of Job in the Bible, the man who lost everything—his wealth, his children, and his health? The term "Job's comforters" is still used pejoratively, describing people whose help is more hurtful than helpful, but if you read the story carefully (and I strongly encourage you to do so) you will see that his friends really did care about Job. In fact, they were so moved by his intense grief that they sat with him, silently, for a whole week, before Job finally felt comfortable enough to break the silence. Note that they let *him* break the silence.

AIDS Lesson 23:

The best thing to say when you don't know what to say is nothing. Simply being there, silently, is far better than saying things that ultimately may prove unhelpful or hurtful.

Sharing this journey silently with Scott was good preparation for walking with others during their struggle with AIDS. I already mentioned Bailey's mother, Susan, the one who said, the first time we met, "The Bible is the cruelest book that's ever been written" This statement was so offensive to my way of thinking that I had absolutely no idea how to respond. So I didn't say anything. I just sat there in stunned silence, trying to figure out what to do next. I struggled with this later, wondering, *Oh, Lord, did I deny You like Peter did by not saying something?*

Over time I learned that my response—silence—had been the best choice in that situation because Susan's unspoken concern, knowing I was a believer, was: *Are you just another of those sanctimonious Christians who feel they have to pass judgment on people like me, my other children, and my son with AIDS? Because if you are, I don't want anything to do with you.*

What she didn't realize was that Bob, Scott, and I had

been on the receiving end of these attitudes ourselves, sometimes from people we didn't know, and sometimes from those closer to us. I'll give you just two examples. In both cases, we wish that if they had wanted to offer support, they had chosen silence as their gift.

Shortly after Scott came home with AIDS, someone from our church came to call. Bob was at the hospital, so Scott and I were alone. I should have known something was up when the visitor lugged in his big Bible and rather stiffly took a seat in the family room across from Scott, who was lying on the sofa.

"Scott," the visitor said, "I want to know how you feel about the life you've been living the past five years."

Scott replied, weakly, with one word, "Deplorable."

"Well," the visitor said, "that's what I came to hear you say."

He stayed only a few more minutes, then announced, "I really need to go to prayer meeting tonight."

After the visitor left, Scott asked me, "Mom, is that all he came here for—just to hear me say that?"

"I don't know." I really didn't, though I had my suspicions.

Scott continued, "Well, I hope he didn't misunderstand me. I didn't mean that all of my life was deplorable. A lot of it was, but I hope he didn't go away reading into what I said."

Here was Scott, dying young. He didn't know how much time he had. But he had many needs, one of which was for people to accept him as a friend and share the pain, perhaps to reminisce or talk about the value of their relationship or maybe to ask if there was something they could do for Scott. The visitor might have asked, "What does it feel like when you know that you're going to die?" Or, "What do you think about late at night?"

109

But this visitor didn't have time for that. He had to get to prayer meeting, after first having his one question answered. In other words, he was so focused on his own agenda that he totally missed the opportunity to minister to Scott. If you read the story of the good Samaritan (Luke 10), you'll see that this kind of attitude isn't new. You'll also see what Jesus thought of it.

Sometime later, Scott was hospitalized again with pneumonia, Bob's father died suddenly of a heart attack, and we had a chimney fire—all on the same night. My stress level was about a twelve on a scale of ten.

During this time, a church woman Scott had never met asked if she could come by and visit. At that point, I hadn't yet learned to say "No," or better yet, "That depends on your agenda." I figured that most people meant well. Didn't we have an obligation to let people express their concern?

Well, my answer to this question changed as a result of this woman's visit. She did express her concern. But after a few pleasantries, she turned to Scott and said, "Well now, Scott, I know that your sin has given you AIDS."

Scott, who was a little more experienced than I in facing such self-righteousness, replied in a gentle but firm manner, "If that's true, then I suppose everybody should expect to get AIDS. Don't you agree?"

"Well," she replied, obviously flustered, "we're all sinners, yes, but . . . there are *different kinds of sins, and homosexuality is the worst.*"

After she left, Scott said, "Mom, I don't know these people. Why do they come here? To see this new curiosity? Or to witness to this homosexual?"

I didn't have the answer to his question, but I can tell you that these situations were very, very painful for me.

AIDS Lesson 24:
In order to be truly helpful to a person with AIDS, your only agenda should be to discover and meet that person's needs.

You do this not by making speeches, but by asking questions. I'm not talking about rhetorical questions designed to bring up the subject that you want to talk about or prying for information, either. For instance, some people like to knock on a stranger's door and ask, "If you died tonight, do you know where you would spend eternity?" Then, if this person embraces the visitor's agenda, he or she is accepted and nurtured in the faith.

In general, this is the same kind of communication that PWAs and their caregivers receive from many sources, including family, some friends, and even parts of society at large. The message is: Once you have repented of the sin that brought this plague upon you, we may choose to care *about* you enough to care *for* you.

My conviction is that, in order to really help PWAs and their caregivers, we need to take the opposite approach; specifically, we must earn the right to engage them in a spiritual dialogue by proving that we care, by listening and then addressing the needs they express.

When Bailey's mother made such cutting remarks about the Bible and the apostle Paul and Jesus, she was testing me. I guess Susan figured that if I was tough enough to take that kind of abuse about something so dear to me, I might be able to help her face the slow dying of her son, who was so dear to her. I learned over time that this was because she knew she wasn't tough enough to face that experience, and she desperately needed the companionship of someone she could trust.

As Bailey lay dying, I stayed with him practically night and day. It was almost like a replay of the grueling experience with Scott except that this time it was someone else's son. Susan would go out for some fresh air, or home to check on her other children, asking me to stay with Bailey.

As time went on and Bailey's time approached, I knew that I couldn't leave this mother alone with her dying son. Susan didn't want her other children to see Bailey in his final days. I remembered how I had felt during Scott's final hours, so thankful for Bob and Wendy and other family members. Susan's home is exactly one hour from my home, so I quickly gathered up some things I would need—my medications, toiletries, my knitting. Just enough so I could camp out there for several days.

Susan told me later she appreciated it more than words could express. In the middle of the night I asked her if I could sing "Amazing Grace" to Bailey. Based on what I knew of semicomatose people, I expected that he would hear me, if not consciously, then in the depths of his soul. And based on what I knew of Bailey and his faith, I knew that he would appreciate it. But based on what she had said, I felt that I needed her permission.

"That would be very nice," she said. And as I got down right next to Bailey and sang softly into his ear, Susan wept.

Later, one of the nurses read to Bailey from the book of John: "Let not your heart be troubled; you believe in God, believe also in Me. In My Father's house are many mansions; if it were not so, I would have told you. I go to prepare a place for you. And if I go and prepare a place for you, I will come again and receive you to Myself; that where I am, there you may be also" (John 14:1–3).

Two days later, Bailey died. Susan turned to me and

said, "Now I need to go, Mignon. My other children need me. Will you stay and wait for the undertakers, and make sure they take good care of Bailey?"

"Of course," I told her. "It would be a privilege." It was the least I could do. But it was also the most I could do, for I too was exhausted.

It seemed like it took forever for the people to come. When they did, I helped wrap Bailey's body in a sheet and move it from the bed to the gurney.

It didn't bother me at all because I kept thinking that if I were Susan, I would want someone to do his or her best for me.

I have no doubt that had I reacted angrily to the sacrilegious comments she made the first time we met, I never would have had the opportunity to walk with her the rest of the way. Susan and I are good friends to this day.

AIDS Lesson 25:

If you want to truly help PWAs (or their family or caregivers), you must walk alongside them (not in front, expecting them to follow, or behind, shouting advice). The best you can do is offer support and trust God with the rest.

Good helpers are good listeners. I must admit that this isn't easy, but I'm better at this now than I was a few years ago, because I've learned that listening isn't just a passive exercise. It involves asking questions designed to keep the speaker talking. These questions I call "openers," because they open up a conversation.

For example, when I sense that a PWA (or caregiver)

is feeling lonely and isolated, I might ask: "Do you have the support you need?" If he or she trusts me enough to speak frankly, the answer will usually be something like, "Not really, I've really been struggling. Frankly, I have no idea how I'm going to make it through this."

Without forcing anything, I might respond, "I often wondered that myself when Scott was dying. A lot of people helped us in one way or another, but over time I found that faith was what really sustained me."

If he or she wants to talk about that, we will. If not, we'll change the subject. Typically, he or she will respond, "I wish I had that kind of faith." When this happens, I'm always glad to talk about how a personal relationship with God is possible for anyone who will come to Him through faith in Christ.

It's not necessary to force the issue. Most PWAs and their caregivers are already thinking about spiritual issues and they *want* to discuss them with someone who will take the time to engage in a dialogue. But the others—those who rush in to deliver a judgmental monologue—are shut off before a single word comes out of their mouths.

Quite often I will hear about someone with AIDS through a secondary source who knows that this person needs help. So I'll pick up the phone and try to open a conversation by saying, "So and so told me about you. I'm calling to let you know that we try to walk alongside people living with AIDS because our own son died of AIDS in 1989 and we know how it is to try to travel that journey alone. I'd really like to visit with you sometime. Would that be okay?"

When I do visit, I go prepared to help in whatever way is needed, and I always keep confidential whatever I may hear or see.

Let me conclude this chapter with a list of things to

say (and things not to say) when you want to help a PWA. These are only suggestions, not ironclad rules. Use creativity and sensitivity as you try to customize your words to the needs of the person, remembering that in all these things you are only trying to find many ways to say: "I love you, and I care."

Things to say:
- I'm sorry.
- I care about you.
- I'd like to be your friend.
- Please help me understand how you feel.
- Is there any question that keeps coming into your mind?
- If this happened to me, I think I might feel (angry, upset, etc.). Is that how you feel?
- Do you have the support you need from your (friends, family, church)?
- When I pray for you tonight, is there something you would like me to ask God about?
- Do you need anything I could bring you the next time I come?

Things not to say:
- I know how you feel. (You can't, unless the person tells you.)
- How did you get AIDS? (What difference does it make?)
- All things work together for good. (This misuse of a Bible verse is not much help in the face of AIDS.)
- Call me if you need something. (They won't, unless they are truly desperate, in which case you should drop everything and go.)

Suggestions for Caregivers

1. Expect your PWA to ask hard questions that you cannot answer. It's okay to say, "I don't know," especially if you are willing to engage in further dialogue, in which case you might say, "I don't know. What do you think?"

2. Realize that your PWA may not actually be looking for an "answer" to a particular difficult question but simply seeking someone who will respect him or her enough to listen. For example, many hurting people ask the question "Why?" in one form or another. If the response they get is "It's a mystery," they may feel shut off. If you say, instead, "That's a very good question, and one that even Jesus asked. Can we talk about it?" you may keep the dialogue going and in the process learn something yourself.

3. Don't be surprised if the person you are trying to help tests you with some outrageous statement(s), as Susan tested me. This person needs to know if he or she can entrust even deeper things to you. In situations like this, you might say, "I appreciate that you trust me enough to tell me how you really feel. I want you to know that nothing you could do or say could change the fact that I care very deeply about you."

4. Make silence your friend. Being with someone in silence is far better than filling the air with meaningless words.

Suggestions for PWAs

1. Expect people, especially religious people, to say stupid and sometimes judgmental, hurtful things to you. When this happens, don't strike back. But if you must respond, you might remind them that Jesus said, "Let him who is without sin cast the first stone."

2. Resist your need to test the love level of each person who offers to help you. Some of these potential helpers may be discouraged and withdraw their offer if they don't understand the dynamics of your response.

3. If someone says "Call me if you need something," don't be afraid to take the person up on the offer. The person probably doesn't realize how having to ask for help can increase the recipient's sense of obligation and humiliation.

4. Likewise, if someone offers to help with something, let him or her, because by doing so you are giving the person a chance to share in the challenges of your journey, even if neither of you can do much to change the ultimate outcome.

What to Do When You Don't Know What to Do— Seven Keys to Becoming a More Effective Helper

11

Bruce grew up in my hometown. We were neighbors. He spent many happy childhood hours with my brothers, sisters, and me. He came from a loving Christian home.

In January 1993 I received a letter from Bruce's eighty-year-old mother, Elizabeth. "Mignon," she wrote, "I knew you would understand. Bruce has AIDS. Bruce is so loving and kind, he would never hurt anyone. Why has this awful thing happened to us?"

The letter went on, telling about her loving son and his many fine qualities as well as his strong Christian faith . . . and her own extreme sadness about the AIDS diagnosis. The underlying theme of that letter was a mother's deep love. She wanted to do whatever she could to encourage Bruce and walk the journey with him.

Elizabeth was already a seasoned traveler in many ways. Her faith had been tested often. She had lost three other children to death. Her husband had died of cancer several years earlier. But this, she knew, would be the ultimate test.

Bruce lived about two years after he told his mom he

had AIDS. They were good years. He experienced some good health, for which he gave thanks to God. His faith and trust in God grew, but the time came when he was ready to die.

Toward the end, Elizabeth came to stay with Bruce and his companion of nineteen years. At the end of each day she would pray with Bruce. At times she didn't know how to pray. Sometimes all she could manage was that prayer she had prayed with him so often as a child, "Now I lay me down to sleep. . . ."

The last time I talked to Bruce was about two weeks before he died. He told me he wanted to go. He was ready. They all were ready. Bruce's brothers came to see him, along with some cousins and other friends. Bruce died peacefully at home, in the arms of his mother, who had come to help him when he needed her most.

By contrast, Donna Scofield, an HIV/AIDS volunteer from Yakima, Washington, sent me this account of another young man's death:

> The young man cried for his mother the night before he died, one of the other volunteers told me, and my heart broke for him. He was only twenty-four, but life had hardened him with poverty, drug abuse, prison, and for the first few months I had known him he had been stoic, covering his fear with a veneer of bravado. Then as he hung on and on, his body seeming to hold off death with a will of its own, the tough-guy mask disintegrated. Early in the evening he had called out "Mama!"—the first time in weeks he had spoken. Later, around midnight, a nurse checked on him and found him crying softly. A few hours later he was dead.

> All of us in the buddy group had visited him in the hospital, brought roses from the garden and cartoon books, tempted his appetite with his favorite hamburger gravy on mashed potatoes. But none of our faces was the

one he hungered for. The few times his mother visited him, his thin face glowed, and he lay in peaceful silence while she sat in the room. During the last two weeks of his life she simply refused to visit, leaving him to call "Mama" in those final hours, with only his tears for company.

AIDS Lesson 26:

If you want to help a PWA, you must be there, be there, be there. Be proactive. Go to that person. This is the first key to being an effective helper. [1]

In your journey with AIDS, many times you may not know what to do. But your helping will always be more effective if you begin with the end in mind. This is the second key.

The best end (or goal) to keep in mind is that when the end comes for your loved one, he or she will die in peace. In order for this to occur, reconciliations usually need to happen—interpersonally and intrapersonally (within that person). These take work, but their value far outweighs the cost.

In one case a certain father I'll call Stewart never knew that his son, Allen, was gay until the son's companion called to say that Allen had AIDS. Stewart was so grief-stricken by this totally unexpected, double-barreled blast that when I first met him he was almost totally nonverbal about it. I shared that my son had been gay, too, and that he had died of AIDS, so I understood some of the issues involved. Each time we talked during the next few months, Stewart opened up more and more.

Allen's mother's method of coping was to run away.

She would leave, sometimes for days at a time, leaving Allen's care to his father. I told Stewart I was so proud of him for doing this, because Allen needed a lot of attention. I saw Stewart grow to where he went from helping Allen to the bathroom to finally in the last month getting in the shower with him. Allen's AIDS forced a lot of interpersonal bonding in a big hurry. This is one route to reconciliation.

For many PWAs, the intrapersonal issues (the unresolved issues in their hearts and souls) are as important as the issues they've had with other people. Quite often PWAs struggle with a deep sense of inner alienation, usually because the lifestyle that has brought their infection was a violation of the moral standards they were taught as a child. While some counselors might suggest that the way to resolve this inner alienation is to throw off those "antiquated" standards, I have not yet met a PWA who actually achieved a sense of peace through this approach.

As far as I can see, it is an exercise in futility for people to try to resolve their guilt by redefining the rules after their conscience has been violated. You may be able to pull a nail out of a two-by-four, but you can never pull out the hole. It's the same way with guilt.

Remember the story of the Old Testament king, David (the one who wrote a lot of the Psalms), who committed adultery with Bathsheba, and then, once he learned she was pregnant, arranged to have her husband put on the front line of a battle so he would die? David wrote:

> *When I kept silent [about my sin], my bones grew old*
> *Through my groaning all the day long.*
> *For day and night Your hand was heavy upon me;*
> *My vitality was turned into the drought of summer. Selah*
> *I acknowledged my sin to You,*
> *And my iniquity I have not hidden.*

I said, "I will confess my transgressions to the LORD,"
And You forgave the iniquity of my sin. Selah (Ps. 32:3–5)

Guilt brings dis-ease. Forgiveness facilitates peace. There is no better way because there is *no other way*. I have known many PWAs who died in peace after taking this approach. I have not known any who died in peace, spiritually speaking, without taking this approach.

Jonathan had been raised in the Episcopal church. He went through Sunday school. He knew Christ as his Savior. But because of his struggles with homosexuality, he was made to feel that God no longer loved him. I saw him grow spiritually from the time I met him until he died about a year later. We had many long talks about the love and compassion and faithfulness of Jesus Christ. Sometimes we would also talk about the questions of sin and guilt and forgiveness. When we did, I was always careful to include myself in the same category as Jonathan—a sinner saved by grace.

Jonathan taught me a lot about how to dialogue honestly and openly with people facing his issues. Evidently, I was able to help him too. Here's what he wrote to me:

Dear lady,
You have touched me deeply in an area of my heart I feared had died. Your love, your song, and your spirit [have] made an impact on my short life and left me longing for more. In your smile I'm renewed, and in your voice I'm reminded of my home in the sky. May you always know peace and joy and that you are loved and cherished and that you've made a difference in this pilgrim's journey.

My love to you in Christ,
Jonathan

What I recall most about Jonathan, though, was not only the simple integrity of his communications. I remember his eyes. When I looked into his eyes, I saw the eyes of Christ looking back at me. I had seen this before, in Scott, and I've seen it since in other PWAs who were dying. It's hard to explain what I see, but it looks like love and peace, and it draws me toward a reality that transcends anything else I've seen in this life.

AIDS Lesson 27:
As you focus on the goal of helping PWAs find their personal peace, you may glimpse eternity through their eyes.

The third key to effectively helping a PWA is to put first things first. This keeps the main thing the main thing, which is crucial because the journey with AIDS has so many twists and turns.

The main thing is to find the "open door" into the PWA's life—which will usually be one of his or her needs. My belief is that when helpers are willing to walk through this door and address that need, whether it is physical, emotional, financial, or sociological, we will often earn the right to share with that person about even deeper needs.

The safest place to start is with the PWA's physical needs, since these are the easiest to discern. I usually start with simple things like "I'd like to bring some food along. Does anything sound good to you?" Quite often they will say, "I haven't been eating much lately," which tells me that they could be wasting away and need some easily prepared (because they are too tired to do much more than warm something up in the microwave) and digestible foods.

But I never force it. For example, here's an exchange to avoid: "I'm going to make you a pot of chicken soup."

"Well, you know," the person replies, "chicken soup doesn't settle too good."

"Well, you will love my chicken soup because it's the best."

I learned through Scott's experience not to tell a person with AIDS what he or she would love. My friend Gretta would visit Scott and see him sitting at the kitchen counter, weak and maybe eating a little yogurt.

Gretta, who really wanted to help, would say, "Scott, I want to go home and fix something for you. What sounds good?"

"Gretta, nothing sounds good."

"Well, how about some pasta? You always used to like that."

"Gretta," Scott would finally say, "the only reason I eat is because I have to eat. Nothing sounds good."

Even when something does sound good, however, I have this simple advice: *Never stock up*—because for a PWA, today's craving may be tomorrow's nauseating food. Once Scott had a craving for lemonade. So I stocked up on lemonade. But the following day lemonade didn't sound good anymore and he went on to something else.

Likewise, it's frustrating to try to cook ahead. If nothing sounds good and they don't want to eat, you're going to have to let them not eat. That's hard for a caregiver, but it's a violation of a PWA's rights to tell him what he has to eat. He knows what's happening to his body and what he wants or doesn't want. One of the things PWAs most want is respect. Give them this, plus a few homemade chocolate chip cookies, some yogurt, and some peaches (for some reason PWAs often like peaches), and you may discover that they will nibble on the food you brought after you leave.

When you take a similar approach (find the open door and enter there, respectfully) to spiritual things, you may discover that a person who was not much interested is now hungry to know more. This is what happened with Rachel, a thirty-one-year-old college graduate, paramedic, and former lifeguard who has AIDS. Rachel had attended a conference where I had spoken. She had seen the quote next to Scott's photo: "I lost it all to find everything, Jesus my Savior." She knew she needed help in order to face her journey with AIDS. "This is what I'm looking for," she told me. "The things that are giving you strength are what I want for my life. I know my children are going to have to bury me. I know someone else is going to have to raise them, and I want to instill in them Christian qualities and nurturing."

AIDS Lesson 28:

Look for the open door of need in the PWA's life. Respectfully enter this door and address that need, and you may earn the right to help that person address his or her other needs also.

The fourth key to being an effective helper is to think win/win. This is crucial for helpers who want to frame everything in spiritual terms, in which case they will probably come across as self-appointed experts, there to offer a superior perspective on what is going on. The problem is, as someone has noted, "People do not care how much you know until they know how much you care." PWAs need love—no strings attached. When you give it, they win, and you do too. When you don't, everyone loses.

I heard about a church which had seemed open to a certain PWA's attendance until he shared publicly about his ongoing struggles with homosexual orientation. After that, the pastor was told that this person should not be attending the Wednesday night prayer service.

The clear message the PWA got was that if he would become like that congregation—keeping his distasteful struggles to himself—he could become a "winner." Until then, he would always be a "loser" (from their perspective).

The problem was that he wasn't like them, had never been, and still struggled because he longed for intimacy and acceptance from somebody. Instead of trying to create a situation where mutual growth could occur, this group offered conditional acceptance, which is ostracism to the one who cannot meet the conditions. In this case, both sides lost the opportunity to learn from each other.

Before homosexuality and then AIDS came to our home through Scott, I confess I might have classified our family as "winners" compared to those whose less-than-righteous lifestyles demonstrated that they were "losers." Now, I'm convinced that we're all just fellow pilgrims in the process of discovering who we are, what life is about, who God is, and how He is working in our world today. Everyone wins if we can take this one step further and discover how He is working in and through our journey together with AIDS.

When Scott was out of our lives and lived away from us, we were advised by some church leaders not to allow him to come back home. Had we heeded this advice, I would be in the "Home for the Bewildered" today—this is my dear friend Barbara Johnson's term. In fact, it was Barb who helped Bob and me through the very difficult homosexual years. Barb has a ministry to parents of homosexuals called *Spatula Ministries*, located in La Habra, California. She has helped thousands of families, and we are among them. It was she who said, "Mignon, love that boy. God will bring him back." And God did bring our Scott back to us and to Him. We welcomed our son home with open arms, and God did the rest. Scott was so happy to have our relationship healed, and so were we. It wasn't difficult at all to literally put the past behind us, moving forward together in love. *This is winning.*

One of the horrors of this dreaded disease is blindness. Scott would say to me often, "Mom, I just hope I don't lose my eyesight." At that time, we didn't know anyone personally who had gone blind due to CMV retinitis, but we knew about the infection and knew if left untreated, CMV retinitis would progress to bilateral blindness.

Many of my dear friends suffer with CMV retinitis. They take several different medications trying to halt its progression. Some become totally blind, others are in a holding pattern, yet others hang on to just a bit of eyesight. In the face of blindness, I see them tackle this huge obstacle a bit at a time with victory.

Recently I was talking with Adam on the telephone. Adam has lost most of his eyesight. He asked about Arianna and how her recent eye surgery had gone. He said, "When you talk to her, tell her to call me and we can play 'Three Blind Mice' on the telephone!" What victory in the face of defeat! *This is winning.*

I said, "Adam, you are so determined not to let this disease get the best of you! I'm so proud of you and glad to have you for a friend!"

He replied, "Mignon, I couldn't do it without your support and the support of my other friends. You give me the hope and encouragement I need."

This is what can happen when you think win/win. But in order to do this, you must lay aside your expectations, self-righteousness, and a lot of your security, and learn to love the other person fully and from the heart. This is much more easily said than done, but it can be done. It is what Jesus did for us, and what we can do for each other, as the apostle Paul wrote:

> *Let nothing be done through selfish ambition or conceit, but in lowliness of mind let each esteem others better than himself. Let each of you look out not only for his own interests, but also for the interests of others. Let this mind be in you which was also in Christ Jesus, who, being in the form of God, did not consider it robbery to be equal with God, but made Himself of no reputation, taking the form of a bondservant, and coming in the likeness of men. And being found in appearance as a man, He humbled Himself and became obedient to the point of death, even the death of the cross. Therefore God also has highly exalted Him and given Him the name which is above every name, that at the name of Jesus every knee should bow. . . . (Phil. 2:3–10)*

Because Jesus had the mind of a servant, He made winners of all who would receive Him as Savior. In return, God made a winner of Him. When the same "mind" is in us, we are able to achieve a mutually beneficial win/win relationship with others, including PWAs.

AIDS Lesson 29:

AIDS, which appears to be a situation where everyone loses, can be the context for mutual growth and discovery where everyone wins.

The fifth key to effective helping is to seek first to understand, then to be understood. This is just the opposite of the way most PWAs are treated. Others, especially religious people who think they understand, offer pat answers to questions nobody is asking. For this reason, the church's response to AIDS has remained basically irrelevant.

In his book, *The 7 Habits of Highly Effective People*, Dr. Stephen Covey illustrates this point:

Suppose you've been having trouble with your eyes and you decide to go to an optometrist for help. After briefly listening to your complaint, he takes off his glasses and hands them to you.

"Put these on," he says. "I've worn this pair of glasses for ten years now, and they've really helped me. I have an extra pair at home; you can wear these."

So you put them on, but it only makes the problem worse.

"This is terrible!" you exclaim. "I can't see a thing!"

"Well, what's the matter with you? Think positively."

"Okay. I positively can't see a thing."

"Boy, are you ungrateful!" he chides. "And after all I've done to help you!" [2]

PWAs would not go back to a doctor like that (nor would you), so don't force them to look at their situation through any glasses other than the ones God has given them.

Most PWAs long for somebody to try to understand them. If you really will do this, you may be the first person who ever has. This in itself would make the effort worthwhile, but the real reward comes from the in-depth, person-to-person connection (or to use a more spiritual term, *communion*) you may experience together as a result.

AIDS Lesson 30:
The quality of your relationship will grow as you seek to understand instead of first insisting on being understood.

This new relationship spawns what Dr. Covey calls "synergy," which empowers two to accomplish more together than what they might have accomplished as individuals. This is the sixth key to really helping someone in the face of AIDS. Its importance is described well in this Old Testament text:

> *Two are better than one,*
> *Because they have a good reward for their labor.*
> *For if they fall, one will lift up his companion.*
> *But woe to him who is alone when he falls,*
> *For he has no one to help him up.*
> *Again, if two lie down together, they will keep warm;*
> *But how can one be warm alone?*
> *Though one may be overpowered by another, two can withstand him.*
> *And a threefold cord is not quickly broken. (Eccl. 4:9–12)*

The journey with AIDS is lonely. No one can face it alone. Two can help each other. The "threefold cord" may be the writer's way of describing two friends plus the Lord. This is the best route.

This synergistic approach has many benefits, but let

me just mention two. The first is creativity, which I think is God-given and helpful when you're trying to decide what to do when you don't know what to do.

I've been able to use my rose garden to bless PWAs. Through Scott and many other PWAs I realized how they appreciate beautiful flowers, even more so if you have grown them yourself. So, soon after I began visiting people with AIDS, I began taking along some roses from my garden. This impressed Tyler, who had been a florist. When I learned this, I invited him to our daughter Wendy's wedding. He made some nice comments about the flowers. But the best thing about the experience was that it brought Tyler back into church, which had been an important part of his life, at least for that short time. He sat there, taking in all the beauty of the occasion.

The second benefit of synergy is that it energizes. I come from a family that loves to sing. We love music! When I was growing up in a little village in southwestern Minnesota, it was customary for Mother, Daddy, and all six children to gather in the music room on Sunday afternoon and sing Southern Gospel music, specifically Blackwood Brothers Quartet music. We all found our parts, and with my mother at the piano, we made beautiful music!

Since my growing-up years, I have always been involved in singing. Bob has a beautiful baritone voice, so music became a part of our home as well. Scott was a very gifted musician and both of his sisters, Heidi and Wendy, are musical. We sang around Scott's bedside as he made the transition from earth to heaven.

So when I became involved in the AIDS ministry, it was only natural that I use music as a healing balm for the person living with AIDS. Since I am very limited on the piano, *very* limited, I use background tapes. Have tape, will travel; that's me!

I have sung to those on their deathbeds, sometimes when they were comatose, but I also sing for them when they are enjoying reasonable health. I discovered that my singing seemed to bless my friends with AIDS. They especially enjoy songs about heaven, and grace, and forgiveness.

I'm glad that my singing these songs is so appreciated, but what my audience doesn't realize is how much I am strengthened by being able to share this gift with them.

AIDS Lesson 31:

One plus one can accomplish more than two separately. One plus one plus God can provide unbreakable strength.

The final, seventh key, is that you learn to "sharpen the saw." This comes from the idea that if you have to cut down a whole forest, you'll do it more efficiently if you stop from time to time and sharpen your saw instead of cutting nonstop.

In our context, this means that you will be a better helper if you adopt the attitude of a learner, and take time for renewal. Perhaps you've heard this wise saying, "The bow that is always bent will break." AIDS, as much as any other stressor I know of, has the capability of keeping you always stressed . . . unless you can find a way to renew your strength.

You may have to force yourself to do this. Find humor along the way. Scott and I loved to laugh together. You can't do AIDS twenty-four hours a day. Remember this—if you break emotionally, physically, or spiritually, you will be less able to help that person over the long haul, which your journey with AIDS is going to be.

So . . . I'm giving you permission. Take a break, long enough to renew yourself. It's a must. In the next chapter we'll talk about how to go about it.

Suggestions for PWAs

Be patient. Your caregiver may be facing some very difficult issues for the very first time (just as you are). If you can give him or her permission to take a break from time to time, you and your caregiver will be better off. Specifically, give him or her permission to pursue a little personal renewal, even if it is possible that you may die during that time. This will be more freeing to your caregiver than almost anything you can offer.

Suggestions for Caregivers

Review these seven keys, and try to mesh each of them with your style and situation.

1 Be proactive.
2. Begin with the end in mind.
3. Put first things first.
4. Think win/win.
5. Seek first to understand, then to be understood.
6. "Practice synergy."
7. Learn to "sharpen the saw."

How Can We Get Through This?

 **12**

Every mother I've ever talked with whose child is HIV-infected has asked me, "Mignon, how did you get through this?" What they're saying is "I don't know *how* I'm going to survive this. But if you did, maybe there's hope."

Yes, there is hope. That's what this book is about (in addition to faith and love, three qualities which are inseparable).

"I know what you mean," I respond. "When I was walking the journey with Scott, there were times when I wondered if I would make it myself. Frankly, had it been up to me to make it on my own strength, I never could have done it. But I believe faith links us to a source of power outside ourselves, that is greater than anything that may threaten to overwhelm us. I'm speaking of God, of course, who became very close to me and I to Him because of, and not in spite of, this experience."

This fact has more to do with God than it does with me, which I want to make perfectly clear before I go any farther into this chapter. The *only* reason we emerged from this ordeal intact was faith, and the only reason we continue to immerse ourselves in the ordeals of others is because our sense of calling (which also comes from faith) compels us to comfort others with the comfort we have received.

Outside the context of faith in a living God who shares our sorrows and carries us through them when we reach the end of ourselves, I had and have nothing of substance to offer anyone. But because I choose to keep walking by faith, I keep learning the truth of the apostle Paul's words, "I can do all things through Christ who strengthens me" (Phil. 4:13).

Before Scott's illness I knew this intellectually, but it's an entirely different thing to come to know it experientially (which is really the only way to know anything worth knowing). I remember a particular low point, right after Scott's membership had been dropped by the leadership of our church. For generations our family had been part of this denomination, so when they dropped our son, it felt to me like they had also dropped me. I was devastated, desperate for help. For days I tried to resolve my sense of rejection, abandonment, judgment, plus all the angry, defensive emotions that welled up in response to that, like a geyser tapping a giant underground septic system. It was brutal.

I prayed and read my Bible, trying to deal with this. One day I walked through the house, looking up toward heaven, sobbing. "Jesus," I cried out, "somehow help us. Just help this family."

When I did that, a peace came—not instantly, but there was peace. I am confident it was Jesus Himself ministering to my heart. He had let me reach the end of my own strength so I could learn everything I needed to know to carry me through what lay ahead. I didn't hear a voice or see a bright light. Bells didn't go off. But in my heart I knew something in a way I had never known it before that moment: God was in control, and He would be my strength.

This theme permeates the Scriptures, both Old and New Testaments. The Old Testament prophet Isaiah put it this way:

> *Have you not known?*
> *Have you not heard?*
> *The everlasting God, the LORD,*
> *The Creator of the ends of the earth,*
> *Neither faints nor is weary.*
> *His understanding is unsearchable.*
> *He gives power to the weak,*
> *And to those who have no might He increases strength.*
> *Even the youths shall faint and be weary,*
> *And the young men shall utterly fall,*
> *But those who wait on the LORD*
> *Shall renew their strength;*
> *They shall mount up with wings like eagles,*
> *They shall run and not be weary,*
> *They shall walk and not faint. (Isa. 40:28–31).*

AIDS Lesson 32:

Personal faith in the everlasting Creator God enables the weak to gain strength for their journey, wherever it takes them.

In the previous chapter, we talked about the need for personal renewal if we are going to complete our journey with AIDS, which is like finishing the marathon. Notice that in the text above, Isaiah implies that while all who wait upon the Lord can renew their strength, some will rise up with wings like eagles, some will run and not grow weary, and some will walk and not faint. I suppose that had he kept going, he might have added that some may even crawl, but they'll make it if they don't give up.

Most caregivers for PWAs who have learned to practice this passage's operative concept—waiting on the Lord—can locate themselves somewhere on this continuum, though not many I've known would say that they have often soared above the agony. Some run. Most walk, though they may sometimes feel like they can't go on. Some crawl, just barely surviving. I've done a little of each.

Scott was hospitalized eighteen times in the fourteen months after he returned home, including his final stay in the hospital, which lasted three months. I tracked all these stays and other pertinent information on a calendar. Looking at that calendar now, I see a fourteen-month-long emotional and physical roller-coaster ride, without the occasional exhilaration such a ride might provide (not to mention little relief from the occasional vertigo).

After only a month home, Scott hit a major twist and turn. He was already wasting rapidly. Dr. Siegel, his infectious disease physician, said, "I want you to weigh him every day, write down the weight, and report it to me."

Next we did the corkscrew. Scott got an infection, which required hospitalization. While he was in, they decided that in order to combat his rapid wasting, he would have to be put on hyperalimentation,* which meant that he would receive his nutrition through a portacath* which had been surgically implanted into his chest when he was in Century City Hospital. Scott and I called this his "lifeline" because without it he would not have lived.

Unlike most roller coasters, when this one emerged from the corkscrew, we were still upside-down. Scott returned home, needing this same treatment indefinitely. It took twelve hours, so we hooked him up early in the evening and by morning the process was completed. To help him regain weight, we fed him lipids*—pure fat— along with TPN* through the portacath. Eventually he regained thirty pounds.

Things were okay until an infection set in around the portacath. The portacath was removed surgically, which left a gaping wound about four inches long, two inches wide, and about an inch deep. The raw flesh was located high on Scott's chest. My job was to dress the wound daily. Whenever I was in direct contact with the open wound I wore latex gloves. But handling the dressing and the tape was awkward and at times difficult because the tape would stick to the gloves and we'd have an awful time of it. Scott and I would laugh because it was somewhat funny. At some point I started working on it bare-handed, and Scott would always say "Mom, be careful, put your gloves on," which I did, at least until the wound itself was covered. Then I would take off the gloves and finish up. I was always afraid of hurting him or failing to clean the wound properly, leaving his immune-deficient body susceptible to more infection.

During this time, there was so much bonding. We were close again in a way only a mother and child can be. He often said, "Mom, you're more careful than the nurses." I'm not saying that we did everything right, but we did the best we could. One night part of the IV line came loose and we had lipids all over the bed. Several times the line itself got plugged up. Except for the people from home-health care who checked in with us from time to time, we had to handle all these things ourselves. This drew us together. We laughed, we cried, and we talked. We talked a lot.

When the wound finally healed up, the scar it left was

140

the shape of a perfect cross. I said, "Scott, the Lord has left you with a scar as a reminder of Him." He was proud of that scar, and I was proud of the way he handled it.

AIDS Lesson 33:
AIDS is a roller-coaster experience in which caregivers, especially parents, have a choice—ride to the end, or get off before the ride is over. If you choose the latter, somebody will be hurt. If you choose the former and strap yourself in with the seat belt of faith, you will always treasure the memories you make.

As should be obvious by now, I have only one thing to say in this chapter, so I hope you will oblige me if I say it again in a different way: The only way through the agony of AIDS is in the strength that faith provides. This strength is not, thankfully, a one-time allotment. It is a *renewable* resource, something that happens by choice, not by chance, and must involve the whole person.

Most of us know these principles of healthy living:

- Get proper nutrition.
- Get enough sleep.
- Exercise.
- Don't smoke.
- If you drink, do it moderately.
- Cut back on caffeine.
- Reduce stress.

For some caregivers, AIDS is an invitation to violate all of the above principles, plus some I haven't mentioned.

Not only that, compared to the "health" of the PWA, it's easy to view your own health as inconsequential.

But just imagine a certain mother, whose son is hospitalized, dying of AIDS. In order to see her son before work, this woman drags herself out of bed at 5 A.M. every day after five hours of rather fitful sleep (because the only way she can get to sleep is with a very stiff nightcap). She washes down a couple of jelly donuts with three cups of coffee, after which she chain-smokes her way to the hospital, a trip that ties her stomach in knots every time she makes it. Her son begs her to stay, but she can't. She has to work to pay the bills. She promises to return after work, which involves a commute through very heavy traffic. By the time she does make it back, without stopping for supper, she is totally beat. But she pastes on a happy face and walks into the room to be greeted by the same thing he says every night, "I missed you, Mom. Couldn't you come sooner?" She wants to scream, and she wants to cry, but she doesn't have the energy for either.

This woman is heading for a physical breakdown if this pattern continues. Difficult as it may be to do, she needs to see her physician, who will prescribe a more healthy pattern. Then she needs to explain to her son: "I am here for you because you need me. And I want to be here for you next month or next year when you may need me more. My doctor says that if I keep up this pace and pattern, I am headed for a breakdown. So, because caring for you means I have to care for me, I'm making some changes. I'll visit you on weekends and after work each night. But I'll leave at eight so I can stop at the Y and swim some laps before I go home. I can't come in the mornings before work, because I have to get more sleep and eat a good breakfast and maybe even take a little walk around the block, and there isn't time for everything."

AIDS Lesson 34:
If you're going to finish this long-distance race, you must take care of the only body that can take you there—your own.

Emotional renewal is also necessary, but equally difficult, because it requires honestly facing and resolving the many negative emotions I've already written about, such as anger (and its tamer substitutes, disappointment, frustration, irritation, etc.); fear (and its corollaries, anxiety and tension), loneliness, and depression.

If you have one or more of the following nine signs of depression, you need to see a physician immediately because good medication is available today to help. You may resist this suggestion because you think that depression is a sign of weakness. The fact is, many people in long-term stress develop a biochemical deficiency. If you were diabetic, you wouldn't feel guilty about taking insulin. So don't feel guilty about getting help with this. Here are the signs:

1. A pessimistic outlook or gloomy mood most of the time. You may think or say, "I just don't care anymore." You may have sadness that won't go away, no matter what.
2. Loss of pleasure or interest in things you used to enjoy, such as gardening, getting dressed up and going out, preparing and eating good food, sex.
3. Feelings of worthlessness and excessive guilt. A symptom of these would be low self-esteem, constant apologizing for everything, or unnecessary hand-washing.
4. Sluggishness. Does everything seem slowed down? (Some people have the opposite symptom, constant agitation.)
5. Fatigue, loss of energy.

6. Difficulty thinking, concentrating, deciding.
7. Change in weight.
8. Change in sleep patterns.
9. Recurrent thoughts of death.

AIDS Lesson 35:

If you are struggling emotionally, which you most likely are, don't try to tough it out alone. Get help. Your physician should be your first stop. He or she can recognize and treat your depression.

But don't forget that the resolution of these issues usually involves sharing them with others, who will weep with you . . . but also laugh with you. Tempting as it is to withdraw within yourself, or to become absorbed in the needs of your loved one, if you neglect significant others such as your spouse, your larger family, or your close friends, you may come to the end of your PWA's struggle to find yourself facing the rest of your life alone.

The scenario (in terms of marriage) is usually something like this: The PWA comes home, wanting the kind of help that only a family can provide. The parents welcome their child home without realizing all the changes that will occur. Suddenly, their home is transformed into a hospital unit, and their life is no longer their own. The mother, usually the primary caregiver, becomes totally absorbed in the care of the PWA.

The only way to avoid this is to absolutely refuse to allow yourself to become so absorbed in meeting the needs of your PWA that you neglect the others in your life with whom you want to have a continuing relationship after this ordeal is over.

Bob and I discussed this right at the beginning, when Scott told us he was homosexual. Somehow we knew this could have an adverse impact on our marriage and family. During a phone conversation with Barbara Johnson of *Spatula Ministries*, she told us that nearly 80 percent of parents who have a child who is gay end up divorced. Bob and I determined that we did not want to be a statistic. We talked about it openly with each other. We were not going to blame ourselves. I told Bob that he was the best dad Scott could have ever had, that he did nothing to cause Scott to be gay. Likewise Bob told me I was a very good mom. Later Scott confirmed this to us.

Now that AIDS had become a part of our family, we realized that one day Bob and I would have to pick up the pieces. It was scary! We had not lost a child to death and had no idea what to expect, except much pain. I didn't know if I could see this to the end. But we expressed our thoughts and feelings to each other and determined we wanted to come out of this with our marriage and our home intact.

Eight months after Scott came home with AIDS, his health stabilized for a brief period. He mentioned to us that he wished we could take a little vacation. He knew the toll AIDS took on all of us since by then he had had three brushes with death. On one of his doctor visits, he mentioned to Dr. Teays in my presence that he wanted his mom and dad to take a vacation. Dr. Teays was supportive because he was very aware of the stress this disease brought with it. I said I was open to the idea as long as Scott had someone to stay with who could deal with any emergency that might come up. Dr. Teays made the whole vacation possible by offering to let Scott stay with him and his wife, Carol. Bob and I were overwhelmed by their generosity.

We traveled to Japan to see our daughter Heidi and her family, but we assured Scott we would be on the next plane home if he needed us. We were gone for ten days and it was good. Heidi was pregnant with her second child at the time. Later, I was unable to go to Japan when the baby was born because Scott was nearing the end of his journey, so this trip was especially meaningful. While we were in Japan, Scott called, saying he missed us so much. This was so out of character, since he was very independent under normal circumstances, but now everything was different. Much had happened and we all realized how fragile life is. We told Scott we missed him too and would be home soon.

The trip restored our frayed nerves and bolstered our spirits. Because Bob and I were able to get away and enjoy each other and our other children, we were more able to face what was to come. This was a much-needed respite that our dear Scott knew we needed.

AIDS Lesson 36:
In terms of your relationship with your larger family and friends, AIDS will be either a wedge or a glue. Only by consciously, consistently choosing to maintain—even build—these other relationships during your journey with AIDS will you make it a bonding experience.

As I end this chapter, I want to leave you with the most important point: Authentic renewal is an inside-out thing. In other words, it starts in the spirit and works itself outward through the soul (mind, will, and emotions), through the body, all the way into the realm of the relational. It cannot be done in reverse.

Your spirit's renewal is, at its core, a function of the depth of your experiential knowledge of and love for God. This relationship is the key to really living, now and into eternity, and the key to transcending and transforming the roller-coaster experience we call AIDS into an opportunity for growth toward maturity, for both PWAs and their caregivers.

Suggestions for Caregivers

If you want to do more than survive your journey with AIDS, you should:

1. Establish and/or nurture a personal relationship with God. No other foundation will stand up to the storm. A personal relationship with the everlasting Creator God is made possible only through trusting in Jesus as Savior, for Jesus Himself said, "I am the way, the truth, and the life. No one comes to the Father except through Me" (John 14:6). Jesus also said, "For God so loved the world that He gave His only begotten Son, that whoever believes in Him should not perish but have everlasting life" (John 3:16). In another place the same author says, "As many as received Him [Jesus], to them He gave the right to become children of God, to those who believe in His name . . ." (John 1:12).

    If you want to become a child of God, you must receive Jesus as your Savior, by faith, which you can express in a prayer as simple as this: "Almighty God, I need Your help in many ways. First of all, I need to be saved, for I have sinned. I ask Your forgiveness on the basis of the sacrificial death of Your Son, Jesus. At this moment, and from now on, I am trusting in Him alone for salvation and eternal life. I turn away from a life of selfishness and sin, and I hereby commit my will and my life to You. I want to obey You, glorify You, and enjoy You forever. Thank You for welcoming me into Your family. Please strengthen me to face whatever lies between this moment now, and the moment when I meet You face-to-face. Amen."

2. Don't wait until you are completely depleted to actively pursue personal renewal: physical, emotional, relational, and spiritual.

3. If, according to the list of symptoms of depression, you are depressed, *get help*. If you are so depressed that you don't care if you get help, *please* force yourself to pick up the phone and make a doctor's appointment.

Suggestions for PWAs

1. Give your caregiver space to have a life and to stay renewed. Your caregiver will benefit, and so will you.

2. Practice the principles of renewal outlined in this chapter, and you can also be renewed, even if your health is failing. Remember the words of the apostle Paul: "Therefore we do not lose heart. Even though our outward man is perishing, yet the inward man is being renewed day by day" (2 Cor. 4:16).

Did We Do Something Wrong . . . ?

13 The first time we met Carl, he poured out his heart and cried as he told his story. Carl was a pastor. He and his wife were blessed with just one child, a son named Jim.

Just lately Carl had gotten the double whammy: Jim, now grown up, was homosexual, and dying of AIDS. This father blamed himself, asking questions like, *What did I do wrong? Did I do something to cause this?*

Carl, like many conservative parents of PWAs, put himself on trial. He was the accused, the accuser, the judge, and the jury all in one.

Day and night for months, he struggled with this, willing to be guilty if he really was guilty, but not knowing for sure how to think about it. On one hand, his heart told him that he had done everything he could do to raise Jim in the straight and narrow way, both by teaching him right from wrong, and by trying to model the Judeo-Christian values that he had committed his life to teaching others. But another part of him insisted on blaming somebody. The easiest scapegoat was himself.

As Jim got sicker and was hospitalized in California,

Carl drove from another state to visit his son with the goal of reconciliation and expressing his love. Although the visit went well, on the long drive home all of Carl's guilt and confusion resurfaced with a vengeance. *Jimmy is dying. I must have done something wrong. I have lost my credibility as a minister. My reputation is ruined.*

The anguish was so overwhelming, Carl did the only thing that made sense to him at the time—he decided to come clean with his congregation and let them know what he and his family were going through. The following Sunday he shared his heavy burden during his sermon, in which he laid bare his soul.

Unfortunately, Carl's particular church was not quite ready to have such an imperfect person in a leadership position. A church member called the denominational leadership, suggesting that Carl was no longer qualified for the pastorate since his son was gay. In the end, Carl chose to resign rather than fight. He had enough self-accusation to deal with. He didn't need to face the accusations of others who could have been his friends.

AIDS Lesson 37:

If your son or daughter has acquired AIDS through promiscuity or drug abuse, you may feel (or be made to feel) like a failure. False guilt and true guilt feel the same and are not easily resolved, especially if your subculture blames you too.

Most parents do their best to raise their children. I know we did. When Bob and I married in 1957 we set out with goals and hopes and dreams similar to those of many others beginning a marriage and a family in the '50s. We were happy living in a small basement apartment in Spokane, Washington. We might not have had all that the world had to offer, but that didn't matter. We wanted to have a baby and begin our family, like so many of our friends.

Scott was born on the morning of February 4, 1960, after a long, hard labor and delivery. But when I finally held that little boy in my arms, nothing else mattered! He was everything we had hoped and dreamed and prayed for in one precious bundle. I counted his fingers and toes. To this day, I can see Scott's beautiful eyes looking us over too!

We told him how happy we were that he had come to be a part of our family. "Scotty," I told him, "I have waited so long to see you and hold you in my arms, my darling little boy!"

I remember a day when Scotty was about five months old and we were all riding in the car one Sunday afternoon, on the way home from visiting friends. Scotty was sitting on my lap (this was before the days of seat belts). I said to Bob, "I don't know if I could ever love another child as much as I love Scotty."

Bob looked at me, a little puzzled, and said, "Oh, sure you could."

He was right, of course.

Heidi, a beautiful baby girl, was born twenty-two months after Scott. I realized I could love another child just as much! We loved family life. Bob and I fully shared parenting responsibilities. At night after dinner, Bob would do the bath time, giving me a much-needed break from the children, and I would clean up the kitchen. After baths Bob would let Scott ride on his back for what seemed forever! Later it was books, prayers, and then bedtime.

Life was wonderful for us, and we enjoyed our little

family so much. Then fourteen months after Heidi was born, Wendy joined us. Again there was as much love for yet another beautiful little girl! Were we happy? Yes, we were! I just wanted to be the best mommy to these three little gifts from God.

When the children were still young, they learned a Bible verse for every letter of the alphabet, handpicked by their mom to hide in their hearts, verses to give them strength and hope for the future. I list them here in the King James version:

A And all things, whatsoever ye shall ask in prayer, believing, ye shall receive (Matt. 21:22).

B But he knoweth the way that I take: when he hath tried me, I shall come forth as gold (Job 23:10).

C Casting all your care upon him; for he careth for you (1 Peter 5:7).

D Delight thyself also in the LORD; and he shall give thee the desires of thine heart (Ps. 37:4).

E Enter into his gates with thanksgiving, and into his courts with praise: be thankful unto him, and bless his name (Ps. 100:4).

F For whosoever shall call upon the name of the Lord shall be saved (Rom. 10:13).

G Go ye into all the world, and preach the gospel to every creature (Mark 16:15).

H He that overcometh shall inherit all things; and I will be his God, and he shall be my son (Rev. 21:7).

I In all thy ways acknowledge him, and he shall direct thy paths (Prov. 3:6).

J Justice and judgment are the habitation of thy throne: mercy and truth shall go before thy face (Ps. 89:14).

K Keep thy tongue from evil, and thy lips from speaking guile (Ps. 34:13).

L Let us therefore come boldly unto the throne of grace, that we may obtain mercy, and find grace to help in time of need (Heb. 4:16).

M My grace is sufficient for thee: for my strength is made perfect in weakness (2 Cor. 12:9).

N Not every one that saith unto me, Lord, Lord, shall enter into the kingdom of heaven; but he that doeth the will of my Father which is in heaven (Matt. 7:21).

O Oh that men would praise the LORD for his goodness, and for his wonderful works to the children of men! (Ps. 107:15).

P Peace I leave with you, my peace I give unto you: not as the world giveth, give I unto you. Let not your heart be troubled, neither let it be afraid (John 14:27).

Q Quench not the Spirit (1 Thess. 5:19).

R Remember now thy Creator in the days of thy youth, while the evil days come not, nor the years draw nigh, when thou shalt say, I have no pleasure in them (Eccl. 12:1).

S Seek ye first the kingdom of God, and his righteousness; and all these things shall be added unto you (Matt. 6:33).

T The angel of the LORD encampeth round about them that fear him, and delivereth them (Ps. 34:7).

U Unto thee, O God, do we give thanks, unto thee do we give thanks: for that thy name is near thy wondrous works declare (Ps. 75:1).

V Vengeance is mine; I will repay, saith the Lord (Rom. 12:19).

W Whatsoever things are true, whatsoever things are honest, whatsoever things are just, whatsoever things are pure, whatsoever things are lovely, whatsoever things are of good report; if there be any virtue, and if there be any praise, think on these things (Phil. 4:8).

X Examine yourselves, whether ye be in the faith; prove your own selves. Know ye not your own selves, how that Jesus Christ is in you, except ye be reprobates? (2 Cor. 13:5).

Y Yet a little while, and the world seeth me no more; but ye see me: because I live, ye shall live also (John 14:19).

Z Be zealously affected always in a good thing (Gal. 4:18).

When Scott was growing up, he was like most other boys—playing with his toy trucks, baseball, and such. For years our life was filled with birthday parties, Good News Clubs in our home, Sunday school, Boy Scouts, Little League, piano lessons, swimming lessons, and spending time with cousins.

I prayed daily for our children, for God to lead and guide them for the future. When I ran out of things to pray for, I would pray for the person each of them would one day marry. It never occurred to me that Scott would not marry. He was such a loving person and interacted well with girls. In fact, in the first grade, he asked a girl to marry him!

We tried to give our children every physical and spiritual benefit. Older people who had not grown up in Christian homes would comment, "You know, Mignon, your children are going to grow up from baby-hood in a home where Christ is honored and revered. Just think of what they have."

We felt really blessed (and perhaps just a little too proud) of our perfect little family. We'd go to the Cannon Beach Conference Center in Oregon every summer and Scott would stand on a chair and recite the ABC verses he knew so well while his sisters prompted him if he got stuck. When he was six years old he invited Jesus into his heart at that place.

When he was nine he sang his first solo in church— "There Is a Name I Love to Hear." When he was ten he was a soloist in a Christmas program. As a sixth grader he received the American Legion Award. He was a high achiever. He wanted to be the best; number one. He didn't excel in sports but he participated. He was student body president of the junior high. He loved to laugh and had a terrific sense of humor. He got good grades. He was just a good kid.

During junior high and high school his faith really became important. He'd go down to the Safeway parking lot and witness to people. He was very open about his faith. He took voice lessons and received awards and honors for his music, singing lots of solos in concerts at the high school. He was a leader in our church's youth group. Later he attended a Christian college, followed by studies at Capernwray Bible School in England, directing the choir along with doing his studies.

I was so proud of Scott. He seemed to have his life together. Never in my wildest nightmares did I suspect that since junior high Scott had struggled with homosexual desires, which he kept his deepest, darkest secret.

About a month before Scott told us he was gay I was driving in the car, listening to Christian radio as a young fellow told about coming out of homosexuality. *My goodness,* I thought, *I can't believe this guy is talking about something so personal.*

After Scott told us he was gay, I called that station and asked for that speaker's name and address. Among other things, the station sent me Barbara Johnson's address and phone number. Barbara had written a book—*Where Does a Mother Go to Resign?*[1]—which told about her own journey with her son's homosexuality. I knew that Barbara would understand what I was facing. I even thought she might talk to me. So I called her.

Barbara listened and said, "Now, you know, we're just going to wrap that boy up in a comfort blanket of love and give him to God, and let God take care of him." She assured me that God was in control, and that He loved Scott very much. She used words like "your precious boy" and "this darling son of yours." It wasn't a lengthy conversation. She prayed with me and said "I love you." For the first time in awhile, I felt that somebody really understood.

Barbara mailed me some materials, which arrived Christmas Eve. Truthfully, those resources got me through that Christmas, when my whole little dream world had been shattered. I needed someone who had been there to assure me, "You're going to make it."

AIDS Lesson 38:

Even if you raise your child the best you know how, things may not turn out the way you intended. God loves you anyway, and He also loves your child even more than you do.

Love. That's the key to overcoming feelings that you did something wrong (or even that the PWA is to blame). Sincere love.

In biblical times, dishonest merchants would rub wax into the cracks of blemished pottery. But when the discerning buyer held those pieces up to the sun, the cracks were immediately visible. The word *sincere* comes from the Latin *sine cere*, which meant "without wax."

"Love" that is not sincere cannot stand the heat of the HIV/AIDS experience. But sincere love, love that originates with God and flows to others through us, is able to fill up all the caverns of guilt with grace.

This fact is important for the parents of PWAs, not only for their own mental and spiritual health, but also because the experience of receiving grace inevitably leads to bestowing grace on others; specifically, the PWAs under their care.

I've seen many parents who initially chastised themselves as failures because their child had AIDS move beyond that perspective to a deeper love for God, for themselves, and for their child. This deepening love is expressed in as many ways as there are relationships, but I know this transition has happened when parents who initially hid in shame and fear come out of the closet and boldly proclaim to anyone listening that they are proud of their son or daughter.

And rightly they should. For many PWAs are sensitive, kind, discerning, loving, creative, spiritual, and otherwise gifted and appreciated. Does the fact that they contracted AIDS through promiscuity, drugs, or homosexuality mean they should be treated as lepers and outcasts until they die? Possibly, if you mean the way Jesus treated lepers and outcasts. The latter He welcomed and shared meals with. The former, He even dared to touch.

If you have a child with AIDS, and you choose to celebrate his or her good qualities instead of heaping guilt upon guilt, you should not be surprised if some people disapprove of your gracious attitude. They may accuse you of condoning an unacceptable lifestyle, which proves to them that you really are culpable for having caused the child to go astray.

Don't give in to this, because more important to you than the approval of those who think they understand but don't is the approval of One who really does understand and loves you more than you could dare to ask or think.

AIDS Lesson 39:

Love costs, or it isn't worth much. Costly love extends grace to us, and through us bestows grace upon others, to whom this feels like acceptance, forgiveness, even appreciation.

Suggestions for Caregivers

1. You can analyze to death the question "What did we do wrong, that things would turn out this way?" Because you're human, you did some things wrong. But because you are caring parents, you did many more things right. Why not ask instead, "What did we do right, that things aren't worse than they are?"

2. Parental guilt over the sins of a child may be common, but it is not constructive. As Josh McDowell said to me: "We are not responsible for our children. We are responsible to our children. . . . We're responsible to love them, to nurture them, to provide for them, to educate them, to discipline them, to hug them, to love them, to introduce Jesus to them, to pray with them, to introduce biblical principles and lifestyle. . . . But . . . they will make choices that maybe will not be the choices we want them to make and that is not our responsibility. We are responsible *to* our children, not *for* our children."

   In other words, they are responsible for themselves.

Suggestions for PWAs

This is one of the greatest gifts you can give your parents if they are struggling with guilt over what has happened to you: Acknowledge your responsibility for your actions. Forgive them for their imperfect parenting. Agree to keep guilt out of your relationship.

In our case, we apologized to Scott. "We know we weren't perfect parents, Scott, but we did our best," we said. We mentioned some areas where we possibly could have done better. On Thanksgiving, 1988, he emphatically told us: "Mom. Dad. I want you both to know there is nothing you did to contribute to where I am at."

Realize that one reason your parents struggle so is that they wish with all their hearts that they could change your situation. Of course, logic declares that nothing they can do now will change what did or didn't happen then. But this is not a purely logical problem. It is primarily an emotional problem, with which you can help them by saying, "Mom. Dad. I know you tried real hard to be good parents, and I thank you for that. And for the times when you failed, I forgive you. More than anything, I'd like us to start over from right now, today, and build what we can while we still have time."

What Is the Hardest Thing?

14 When Josh was in the final stages of AIDS, his parents were wondering if they should take a trip to Germany. This trip had been planned for some time. It involved meeting some friends there and spending time with them.

Josh's mother called me a couple of days before they were scheduled to leave. "Mignon," she said, "I just have to talk to you. I really think we should cancel this trip."

I said, "Does he want you to go?"

"He says he does, but I don't really know," she replied.

"What if Josh died before you came home?" I asked. "Have you said everything you need to say?"

"Yes," she said. "I think so."

"Then you'll have to get right in his face and tell him if he wants you to stay home, you will."

"I already have, and he says it's okay. He wants us to go."

"Then if there's one thing that you still want to say to him, say it. When you get on that airplane you need to be sure that if you never see him again there was nothing left undone."

While Josh's parents were gone, he became quite sick. After he hadn't eaten for five days he told me, "You know, I'm ready to go. I could go today or tomorrow. I could just say let's get this thing over with except that my mom and dad are not here. I'm not afraid to die. I've taken care of all my spiritual business. I feel I'm going to heaven. But I know that my family is going to grieve and I know that my mom and dad and brothers and sisters are going to be sad. I feel bad that I'm putting them through this."

"But Josh," I said, "they're going to be okay. Your family has a strong faith. That's where their strength will come from."

Then I made it personal. "You know, Josh," I said, "I've really grown close to you during these last couple of years. It's not just because of AIDS; we've become good friends and I'm going to miss you."

He got really choked up and said, "Mignon, thank you so much for telling me that. That really means a lot."

Josh's journey lasted a little longer than we had expected. After his parents returned home, I told his mother one day, "The time is going to come, and you'll know when it's right, to tell Josh that he may go."

"Oh, Mignon," she said. "I don't think I could ever do that. I just don't think I can do that."

"Well," I encouraged her, "you know what you can handle. But when someone is dying, it's really important to release him and let him go." I knew from what Josh had said to me that he was ready. Now it was time for his loved ones to cheer him on.

A few days before Josh died, he tearfully told his mother, who was still hoping for a miracle, "Mom, you know that miracle you've been praying for? Well I'm praying for that miracle. I'm praying that I can go." And then to make her feel better, he added, "And you know I'll see Grandma and my brother."

"Josh," she replied, "if that's your prayer, then that's my prayer too." Later she told me this was her way of giving him permission to go.

Josh lingered another day. At about 6 A.M. on the day he died, when his brothers and sisters and parents were all there, Josh's father said, "Josh, it's okay. You can go now." Josh took several more breaths and he was gone. It was almost as if he had been waiting to hear these words.

AIDS Lesson 40:

PWAs who are dying often need to receive from their caregivers (especially their parents) "permission" to go. This is a difficult thing for any mother to do.

I first encountered this concept when I was picking up a prescription for Scott at the drugstore and I saw the little book *A Gentle Death*. It was the best little book that I could have read. It was about how dying people need control. It gave me so much insight into our situation and prepared me with just the right words, which I said to Scott on July 21, 1989, only a week after his final stay at Whidbey General Hospital had begun.

Early in the morning, he was having such awful stomach and neuropathy pain that the nurse called me at home to say that Scott wanted me to come to the hospital. The methadone cocktails he was receiving were not holding the pain at all.

When I entered his room, it was obvious he was in

great distress. "Do you want me to ask the doctor for morphine?" I asked.

"Yes," he said through clenched teeth. "I just can't keep on like this." I asked the nurses to call Dr. Teays to make the arrangements.

As we waited, he began to relax a bit, probably because he knew I was there and that I would intercede for him. During that time, he turned to me and said, "I just don't know how much longer I can keep going like this."

That was my cue. "Scott, you may go," I replied. "You may go. Heaven awaits you and it's going to be wonderful. Dad and I are going to be okay. We're going to miss you a lot but we have each other and we have our faith and it will be okay. You'll be there to welcome us. It won't be long and we'll all be together eternally. That's the day that we look forward to."

He started to cry and he said, "But, Mom, it's so hard to do."

Not long afterward, Bob came in, having just finished with a meeting. I told him that we were waiting for morphine. As we sat there, Scott turned to Bob and said, "Dad, this is so hard. I don't know how much longer I can keep on."

Bob had read *A Gentle Death* as well. "Scott, you can go," he said, quietly. "We'll be okay."

We weren't saying we *wanted* Scott to go, and he knew that. We were trying to relieve him of any guilt he might feel for leaving us behind. And we were trying to lay a foundation for what was just ahead—only eight weeks ahead.

On Thursday morning, September 14, 1989, I gave Scott his last shave. He'd been bedridden for days, fighting fevers and vomiting, so his beard was a mess. Nobody really wanted to shave him with the instrument of choice, a straight razor. I really didn't think about getting infected from a cut, but I was afraid of hurting him.

We had a very special time as I leaned over the bed. It took a long, long time, but he had a nice clean shave when I finished. I didn't nick him once. But when the razor would pull a little bit I'd say, "Oh, Scott, did that hurt?" And he'd say, "No." It didn't hurt him because by then he was on at least 170 mg of morphine per hour.

Late that afternoon, he got a high fever—104 or 104.5 degrees. I wondered, *Is this going to be it?* We'd had episodes like this before where the fever would be very high one day and then go down right away. But this time would be different. The medical team and Scott had agreed that when the end seemed inevitable, if Scott developed pneumonia, it would not be treated with antibiotics.

By that evening, I began to see a change. It was 7 P.M., my usual time to go home. I was tired. That particular night I said, "Scott, I think I'm going to go now. Your temp is down. I'll be back in the morning okay?"

I went around to the side of his bed and kissed him good night, expecting his usual response, "Okay, Mom," or "That's fine, Mom. Thanks." This time he didn't say anything because he didn't want me to go.

I couldn't talk about this for about two years, because it bothered me so much that I didn't stay. But I was so spent that I couldn't stay any longer. As I've mulled it over, I've come to believe that Scott knew things were happening. He was saying to me, without words, "Mom, can't you tell? I'm going to die. Please don't leave me."

AIDS Lesson 41:
You simply cannot know in advance how things will turn out, especially with AIDS. Accept this in advance.

When I got to the hospital the next morning, Scott couldn't talk anymore. He just looked at me. I knew he could see me and hear me, but he couldn't speak.

We kept a vigil at his bedside all day. That night, we called the family. He hadn't talked and his fever was staying high. The doctors were beginning to tell us that he was probably getting pneumonia. Bob and I spent that night at the hospital.

Then Saturday morning, Bob had to run home to do something. At about noon my tears began to fall. They fell and they fell and they fell. As I was crying, Scott groaned, and I wondered, *Is he saying "Mom, don't cry?"* I didn't know, but I prayed silently, *Oh, dear God, the pain is too great. Only You can ever heal this heart of mine that is now ripped wide open and is bleeding.*

I looked at Scott and wondered, *Are you passing through the valley of the shadow of death? Even though we gave you permission to die two months ago, I didn't know it would be like this.*

He was in pain, and my mother's heart shared it. Bob walked in and out of the room periodically. He brought me coffee. I drank fluids and ate food brought to the room. But I wouldn't leave Scott.

We had unplugged the phone in Scott's room, and our calls were taken at the nurses' station. They said Charly and his mom were going to call at a particular time to tell Scott good-bye. When that time came, I talked with Charly and then said, "I'll put the phone up to Scott's ear."

As Charly was talking, Scott moaned, trying to respond. Pretty soon a tear rolled down his cheek. Nicole, Scott's nurse, was on one side of the bed and I was on the other, and both of us had tears rolling down our faces.

We spent our second night at the hospital. Bob slept in the solarium right next to Scott's room, and I slept in the room. At about 2 A.M., Bob came in to check on us. I said, "Scott, Dad's here too."

Scott looked at Bob and said miraculously and so lovingly, "Hi, Dad." Those were the last words he spoke.

The doctor on call for the clinic came Sunday morning and checked Scott and said, "Well, Scott, I think the chariot wheels are sounding a little louder." So we latched on to that for awhile and said, "Scott, climb in the chariot and go. Let it swoop you up." We began really encouraging him.

Sunday, some of the relatives and Scott's cousins came and they left crying. Scott just hung on even though we were telling him to go.

On Sunday at each shift change the nurses would encourage him. "Scott," they said, "you can go. It's okay. Don't hang on." One of the nurses at the hospital brought us a beautiful fruit tray. It was her day off, but she thought of us and lovingly acted on her thoughts.

Monday they assigned Nicole to Scott as her only patient. He was getting Valium* intravenously every half hour. His morphine was increased as needed throughout the day, beginning at 200 mg per hour in the morning. (When he died eighteen hours later, he was on 530 mg an hour.) The fever and pain raged on, unabated. You could feel the heat radiating from his body.

About 4:30 P.M. Clint Webb, the Baptist pastor, said, "Wendy, take your mom for a little walk." I would shower every day across the hall while we were staying at the hospital those last few days, and get cleaned up there, keeping one eye on the room. I didn't want to go, but I decided ten minutes would be okay.

That evening Clint Webb came again. Since he had been an orderly when he was working his way through seminary, he was familiar with sickness and hospital settings. He put wet cloths on Scott's forehead while we played a musical tape, a collection of many of the songs that Scott had done. Then we played another tape of him singing with a musical group. On one of the tapes there was a trombone solo he played, "I Lost It All to Find Everything."

Then we sang songs like "I've Got a Home in Glory Land" and "Safe in the Arms of Jesus." For a long time we harmonized, just trying to usher him in to heaven. Intermittently we read from the Episcopal prayer book that Father Tench had left with us.

At about 9:30 everyone left and the hospital started quieting down. I said, "Bob, I need to get out of this room for a few minutes. I'll just walk to the front of the hospital and back again." As I came back down the hallway, I could hear Scott's breathing. I prayed, "Lord, must we go through another night of this?" The little walk had done me good, but I was drawn to the bedside of my dying son. Scott · needed me, and I needed him.

Together Bob and I had kept vigil. Wendy had gone into the empty room next door to sleep. Instead of getting into my lounging robe as I had the previous nights, I stayed in my sweater and jeans, hoping and praying that soon Scott's battle would be over.

Later Bob went into the solarium to get some sleep. Scott's breathing became louder. I held my hands over my ears to try to get away from it until I remembered the earplugs in my purse. I felt compelled to stay in that room, but I couldn't take the sound. All the time, Scott had his eyes on me.

At about 11:30, I started writing a letter to Heidi and David, a letter that never got finished. "I'm hoping," I began, "that Scott will go to heaven tonight . . ."

From time to time I got up and stood at the side of his bed. "Scott," I assured him, "if you don't feel forgiven about something, from Dad or me or Jesus Christ, just know that you are, claim that forgiveness, and go."

Still he hung on. Scott had told me two weeks prior that he was ready; there was no unfinished business. So I couldn't think of anything that would be causing this tug-of-war except spiritual warfare.

I put my hand on his head. His eyes were on me as I prayed, "Heavenly Father, I know that you are the only One who can command Satan to release Scott's body, and I ask You in the name of Jesus Christ to do this."

Scott died twenty minutes later. All of a sudden, as I stood by his side, he took a breath and then was quiet. Then he took another breath, followed by a little gurgle in his throat, and he was gone.

I waited to see if there would be another breath, but there was only quiet and peace. With his eyes on me he had gone. I stood there a few minutes in the silence, washed with relief that it was finally over. I was reminded of the Scripture, "For we brought nothing into this world, and it is certain we can carry nothing out" (1 Tim. 6:7).

Softly, I talked to him, "Scott, here we are alone in this room. Dad's in the solarium just steps away. The nurse will tell Dad you died just as the nurse told Dad you were born. Then Dad will wake up Wendy and we will share a precious moment.

"You are finally so peaceful; the struggle is over. My dear, dear son, I am going to miss you more than I could ever have imagined. You taught me how to laugh and find humor in life. You taught me how to be brave and strong and how to claim victory in the face of defeat. You taught me about pain and suffering, so much suffering. You taught me about a mother's love, how far that love goes and how deep. You also showed me how to forgive. Together we learned to trust our heavenly Father more and more as our needs increased.

"Dad and I will go on, and God will be our strength. We will comfort each other. This is your day, Scott, your grand entrance into heaven."

AIDS Lesson 42:

When the end comes, it can be a victory or a defeat. Without faith, it will be defeat. Through faith we can say, "Death is swallowed up in victory" (1 Cor. 15:54).

Suggestions for Caregivers

1. Don't leave anything unsaid. Don't leave any business unfinished. Forgive everything, graciously and from the heart. You will never regret this.

2. Some things may seem too hard to discuss. These may be the most important things to talk through.

3. If your PWA wants to talk about dying or his or her funeral, by all means, listen.

4. Realize that in the end your loved one needs your permission to go. Do not withhold this due to your own needs. Enlist others to help you let go when the time is right.

Suggestions for PWAs

1. You cannot protect your loved ones from the pain they will feel over your leaving, but you can enjoy the source of this pain—their love for you.

2. If you have preferences about your treatment at the end, or how your funeral should be handled, make sure that someone knows them. Realize, however, that your closest relatives may resist dealing with this because in doing so they feel disloyal to you. This, too, is an expression of love. Tell another trusted person, such as a clergyperson, if your family can't face this.

3. Don't leave things unsaid, thinking there will be time later. You don't know how this is going to end. Say what you have to say now.

4. Don't leave anything undone, especially making peace with your family, your friends, and most importantly, God, whom you will probably meet soon. Preparing, through faith, for this meeting should be your highest priority. This is the only way to snatch victory from the jaws of an apparent defeat.

Is There Life After AIDS?

15 You remember Arianna, the former flight attendant who has AIDS. Arianna's mother asked me an interesting question once: "What do you do with your days now?"

This mother, like most mothers of PWAs, could see that Arianna's health was declining. She hated what was happening but felt helpless before it. Based on what she knew about AIDS, she knew that the journey ahead would be a hard one, and she expected that after it was over her life would be aimless and empty. "Arianna is the love of my life," she said, "and I don't know how I'm going to go on without her."

I understood. Scott, Heidi, and Wendy are all the loves of my life, along with Bob. When Scott died, part of me died with him. There was a big vacuum, a hole in my heart that longed to be filled. I knew that only God could heal the hurt. Only He could fill the void.

Over time, He filled it first of all with Himself, and then with a love for people with HIV/AIDS and their families, including Charly, Scott's companion.

The year after Scott told us that he was gay, before he was diagnosed with HIV, he had introduced us to Charly.

Several years later when Scott was home, Charly came to visit him over the Thanksgiving holiday. Charly stayed at a motel a few blocks from our home. Thanksgiving dinner was to be at our home. My mother and some of my brothers and sisters and their families were coming.

"Scott," I said, "if it were just Dad and me and you, Charly could have Thanksgiving dinner with us. But some of the rest of the family might have a problem with this. I think the best thing would be to take a plate of dinner to him in the hotel room."

Here I was a Christian who claimed anyone was welcome in our home, yet my door was closed to Charly. Scott understood, but I'm sure he was hurt and disappointed.

When Scott was hospitalized at Century City Hospital two years later, I was forced to ask Charly for help. "Charly," I said, "can you make some motel reservations for Bob and me? The Century City Plaza is beyond our means."

"Oh, no," Charly said. "You must stay with my mother and me at my mother's house. We won't have it any other way."

"But Charly," I protested. "We don't want to impose. Besides, we need to be able to come and go as we please."

"No," he insisted. "You must stay with us."

This young man whom I, "the Christian," had not welcomed into our home for Thanksgiving dinner, welcomed us into his. That was the beginning of a change, first within me, and then in our relationship. After Scott died, I finally apologized to Charly. "I'm sorry I treated you that way, Charly," I said.

I was so ashamed of the way I had acted that I cried for two hours, even after Charly graciously said, "It's okay. Scott and I didn't do everything right either."

Charly visits us at least once a year, and we have come to love him as a son.

AIDS Lesson 43:

After a person with AIDS has died, those who remain often need to be reconciled with each other. AIDS can drive wedges between people, which need to be removed if those who remain are to experience true healing.

This kind of healing usually comes slowly, as far as I can see. It is unreasonable for a caregiver (or a caregiver's caregiver) to expect the grieving process to "be over" in any particular length of time. This is because in one sense it never can "be over," since the whole experience is now part of you. Not only that, but every person is unique. Some people can get up the next day after their loved one has died, wash their face, comb their hair, and get on with life. Others take weeks. Most take months. Some take years. Whatever it takes is what it takes. This is why the people left behind need so much support, even after their loved one has died.

My own personal recovery still continues. My loss and grief have become my companions. I claim Psalm 27:13, "I had fainted, unless I had believed to see the goodness of the LORD in the land of the living" (KJV). The journey out of AIDS is almost as hard as the journey into it. Along the path, I have stopped for awhile at several way stations. In each place, the Lord has met me in one way or another to let me know when it was time to move on.

For quite awhile I grieved deeply. I hurt all the time.

I was glad Scott was in heaven. But that was a theological certainty, and you can't hug or kiss theology. I missed Scott terribly. We were so close, especially during his final fourteen months. AIDS forced us to become as close again as we had been when he was a child, maybe closer since we could now communicate as adults.

About a year after Scott died, I had a dream that I was driving along through a snowstorm. The car slipped and got stuck in this big bank of snow. I got out of the car to check how badly I was stuck. As I stood there, a car pulled up and a man got out of the car and came to see if he could help me.

"You will have to excuse me," I said, "but you look exactly like my son, Scott."

"I know," he said in a very compassionate way. "And he wants you to know that he has never been happier and that everything is okay with him." I have never seen Scott in a dream since then, but it gave me peace. Maybe God allowed it because He knew that it would help me more than another poem or picture book or song or sermon about heaven.

AIDS Lesson 44:

God gives us what we need in order for our souls to heal. We can resist, or we can cooperate. He leaves that part up to us.

A second major divine intervention came some time later. For the first few weeks after Scott died, I visited the grave every day. Then it became weekly. Later, I would go there perhaps twice a month. I would talk to Scott when I was there, saying how much I loved him and missed him, though of course I knew that he himself was not present.

Last Easter Sunday morning, five years after Scott died, I was driving by the cemetery with Wendy when I glanced over at Scott's grave. A deep groan of grief came from within me. I sensed Scott saying to me, "Don't grieve so hard for me, Mom. Wendy is right there in the car with you. Love her. She needs your love. Enjoy her today. Laugh and enjoy life."

At that very moment, the grief stopped and I lived in the present. I wanted to be healthy and enjoy life. God's message to me was, "Mignon, your life isn't over. Scott worked hard and he was brave, strong, and courageous. His work is finished, but yours isn't. You will find true satisfaction and joy in continuing to help others walk this most difficult journey."

Bob and I had started *Support for the Journey* in response to the need we knew existed. Only two months after Scott died, we had became involved with a couple in Anacortes who were both infected. Bob, Wendy, and I visited this couple on Christmas Eve.

Together with this couple, we decided to begin a support group after the first of the year. We met the first time that February, not knowing that the husband would die in April. They were strong Christian people, and the support had come at just the right time.

Even after the husband died, the group kept meeting. Other people, infected and affected, joined in. Bob and I stayed very active in this group for nearly two years.

I began doing public speaking and supporting people one-on-one. Then in November 1991 a PWA died, and in lieu of flowers his partner asked that donations be given to help people living with AIDS. He asked me to distribute those funds as I saw fit.

As a result of Charly's prodding, we decided that the best way to handle the funds would be to form a nonprofit organization. Two professional people, a lawyer and an accountant, did the paperwork for us pro bono. They also agreed to be on the board. A dentist friend joined our board later. That is how *Support for the Journey* came into being.

We didn't know where this new effort would take us or where we would take it. We've had some effective little fund-raisers, and we're always trying to think of more ways to generate funds to use to address the needs of the steadily increasing group of people affected or infected with HIV/AIDS that have heard about us somehow.

I confess, I love doing the work God has called me to. Actually, I am *compelled* by Christ's love to share that love with others. I can't think of any group that needs to experience this love more than people infected with and affected by HIV/AIDS. Let me tell you about a few more of these friends I've been privileged to know.

Sam was a Lutheran, an outstanding Christian. Sam struggled with homosexuality, so he ended up divorced and separated from his three children. He wrote me, "I wish my mother could see things with the eye of God that you see." Here was a sixty-two-year-old man who was still longing for love from his mother. When it came time for the memorial service, his family requested that it be very private. They hadn't worked through all the issues. The children were ashamed, they didn't want their friends to know about their dad.

John wrote me a whole set of letters. Here's an excerpt from one: "Mignon, you have a fun personality that I've never seen in a mother before. You're a very special woman and I love you so. I feel for you. I don't know how you can be so strong to be here and helping us. You are an outstanding woman."

When I first met John, he was big, heavy, loud, and wearing a T-shirt that advertised condoms. At times he was overbearing, but I knew I had to love him. Over time, John wiggled himself right into my heart.

The facade came down after he heard me sing "There Is a Savior."

"Mignon," he asked me. "Will you sing that song at my funeral?"

I promised that I would.

John had grown up on the streets, prostituting. During the last year of his life, he talked to me about his past, all of which was behind him as he pressed forward toward the prize of eternal life.

"You're okay spiritually?" I would ask.

"Yeah, I'm okay. I'm ready to go. I know I'm going to heaven. I know the Lord is going to meet me when I get there."

"Good for you. Keep at it. Is there anything that you need to talk about or anything unresolved?"

"No. I can't really think of anything."

He died shortly after we had that conversation.

Peter wrote, "Dear Mignon, every person with AIDS needs to have a mother like you. Your example of compassion and strength shames the wicked and blesses the righteous. God bless you abundantly."

Peter was very spiritual and had searched long and hard to find a faith that made a difference. He dabbled in many religions and in New Age philosophy before coming back to his roots, Christianity. Peter had been conceived through his father's extramarital affair. It was a secret until the woman named Peter's father on the birth certificate. One of the nurses at the hospital called Peter's father's home and told his older sister, "There's a baby here. Your dad is the father. If you don't come get him right now, he'll end up in an orphanage."

The oldest sister ran down to the hospital and took Peter home and he grew up in that family. But his step-mother always resented Peter because he was a reminder of his father's promiscuity. In addition, his father didn't know how to love him. So Peter always felt unloved.

A couple of months before Peter died he visited with his family. They never really accepted him because he was gay and dying of AIDS.

All these men had this in common—they craved love and had looked for it in the wrong places. My mission was to show them how to find their heart's deepest longing in the right place: Jesus. Notice I said "show them." I think that in order to earn the right to tell people how to find God's love, you have to model for them first what it is. In this endeavor, I let the simple question "What would Jesus do?" guide me.

If Jesus were here, I know He would listen to them, laugh with them, and weep with them. He would rub their backs and legs, sit with them when they were lonely, and hug them when they were afraid.

He would always be with them. Their fathers or mothers might forsake them, but He would never do that. And after He had been there for awhile, they would ask, "Why are you here?"

"Because I love you," He would say.

"But why do you love me?"

"Because I do, my child. Just because I do."

AIDS Lesson 45:
Jesus loves you, this I know. For the Bible tells me so.

Is there life after AIDS? Yes, there certainly is. My life is fuller now than it ever was before and much more meaningful.

But there is also life after AIDS for the person who dies of AIDS, if he or she will accept by faith that there is a Savior, whose name is Jesus, and embrace Him before passing through the doorway we call death into an eternity of peace, and joy, and love with Him. This truly is God's amazing grace.

Amazing Grace

Amazing Grace! How sweet the sound—
That saved a wretch like me!
I once was lost but now am found,
Was blind but now I see.

'Twas grace that taught my heart to fear,
And grace my fears relieved;
How precious did that grace appear
The hour I first believed!

Through many dangers, toils, and snares
I have already come;
'Tis grace hath brought me safe thus far,
And grace will lead me home.

Appendix A
HIV/AIDS Glossary

AIDS

Acquired Immune Deficiency Syndrome, the life-threatening complications of HIV infection.

blood draws

Blood drawn from a vein for testing.

cytomegalovirus (CMV)

An opportunistic infection that is transmitted sexually and via blood and blood products. CMV can cause fever, malaise, weight loss, fatigue and lymphadenopathy, but in AIDS it is probably just one of several infections that contribute to these symptoms.

CMV retinitis

An infection that generally presents itself with progressive visual field deficits and can cause retinal detatchment. Untreated CMV retinitis will progress to bilateral blindness.

dementia

Can be subtle at first, with difficulties of memory, word finding, personality changes, and motor functions.

Dilantin

A prescription drug that prevents some forms of epilectic seizures.

grand mal seizure

A severe variety of epilepsy marked by convulsions, stupor, and unconsciousness.

HIV

Human Immunodeficiency Virus, which breaks down the body's immune system. HIV infection can give rise to a spectrum of outcomes ranging from asymptomatic infection to full-blown AIDS.

HIV-positive

Persons who test seropositive on a blood test for antibodies to HIV.

hyperalimentation

Synonymous with total parenteral nutrition. *See TPN.*

Kaposi's sarcoma (KS)

The epidemic form of KS associated with AIDS. Usually appears as painless, purple-to-brownish, slightly raised spots on the skin or mucous membranes of the mouth, although the skin lesions may appear anywhere on the body. The gastrointestinal tract is the most common site of internal involvement. The lungs and other organs may become involved, but this usually does not occur until the disease is in its final stages.

lipids

A combination of fats that the body requires for metabolism.

mycobacterium avium complex (MAC)

An environmental bacterium that rarely caused significant infection in humans prior to the emergence of AIDS. MAC infects the blood stream, internal organs, bone marrow, and lymph nodes. The most common symptom is fever. Persons with normal immune system functions are not at risk of developing MAC.

neuropathy

A common neurological syndrome attributed to the direct effects of HIV on the peripheral nerves. It manifests itself by pain, numbness, and tingling of the hands and feet.

opportunistic infections

Infections caused by organisms commonly found in the environment that are resisted by the normal immune system. When the immune system is not functioning properly, these organisms seize the "opportunity" to infect the body.

people with AIDS (PWAs)

People who are HIV infected and have met the criteria for an AIDS diagnosis.

Pneumocystis carinii pneumonia (PCP)

Pneumocystis carinii is a protozoa that causes a slow-developing pneumonia not easily recognized in its early stages.

portacath

A device that is surgically implanted into the body and allows intravenous access to the major veins of the body.

protease inhibitors

A new group of drugs (of different strengths) that fight HIV directly. In order for HIV to cause damage, it needs to reproduce over and over, which takes many steps. The enzyme protease is an important step. HIV needs this enzyme so it can make copies of itself. Protease inhibitors stop the protease enzyme. Like so many things that appear to help fight HIV, there are side effects with protease inhibitors. They are most effective when combined with other drugs.

seizure kit

Five tongue depressors, wrapped together with two-inch gauze and surgical tape, and latex gloves in a Ziplock baggie.

total parenteral nutrition (TPN)

Intravenous feeding that supplies the complete nutritional requirements for proper metabolism, including vitamins, minerals, amino acids, protein, lipids, and sugars.

Valium

A prescription drug used to control anxiety, convulsive disorders, muscle spasms, nervousness, or tension.

wasting syndrome

Characterized by relentless weight loss, fevers, and diarrhea.

Appendix B
Thoughts and Suggestions for Conducting a Support Ministry

1. First and foremost, the person with HIV has to feel safe with you.
2. Listen: Listening is a most important key.
3. Commonality tends to disarm any phobias.
4. Keep confidences.
5. "The disease" is your common bond.
6. Give yourself time to establish relationships. The first time could be uncomfortable.
7. Remember that support is as essential as medicine.
8. People require different levels of support.
9. Walk with them, not in front of them or behind them, but alongside them.
10. Leave the judgment to God.

Appendix C
Suggested Church HIV Policies

Support for the Journey presents these HIV/AIDS policies for review as examples of what others have done. Before you finalize your organization or church's HIV/AIDS policy, it would be wise to have your attorney review it.

A Suggested Policy for Integrating People with AIDS into Your Church Family

The Board of Elders of _____(church)_____ has adopted the following policy on AIDS in the church, which shall apply to the life of the church.

Acquired Immune Deficiency Syndrome (AIDS) is a serious life-threatening condition that is not transmissible by casual contact. The best scientific evidence indicates that AIDS is caused by a virus known as HIV (Human Immunodeficiency Virus), which is transmitted through the exchange of blood or semen by infected sexual partners, contaminated needles, contaminated blood, or by infected mothers to their infants.

Medical knowledge about AIDS is developing, and thus is incomplete. It is almost certainly true that infection with the HIV virus takes a multiplicity of forms, some disabling and some not, varying not only from individual to individual, but also from one phase to another within the same individual. From what is known today, AIDS reduces the body's immune response, leaving the infected person vulnerable to life-threatening infections and malignancies.

In responding to the knowledge that someone attending ____ (church)____ has been infected with the AIDS virus, the Board of Elders will be guided by current medical knowledge, the known behavior of Jesus Christ, and the principles of compassion and ministry established in the Bible.

An individual who has been diagnosed as being HIV-positive or having AIDS should be treated similarly to any other individual attending ___(church)___. In general, ___(church)___ will not reject or ostracize anyone who is HIV-positive or who has AIDS, as long as that individual presents no real threat to the safety of others in the congregation. The confidentiality of HIV-positive individuals will be guarded according to the wishes of the individual.

In the case of infants or small children who are HIV-positive, U.S. Public Health Service guidelines will be followed. Nursery and children's workers will be trained accordingly.

The congregation of ___(church)___ must know that AIDS is not easy to catch. Through appropriate education and counseling the fear surrounding the AIDS epidemic will subside.

It must be noted that in the midst of this tragic epidemic stands our Lord and Savior, Jesus Christ, and His arms of forgiveness, comfort, and healing are outstretched to all people who are worried that they might be positive for the virus or who actually have AIDS, as well as their families and friends.

Confronted with the reality of this modern-day holocaust, the Board of Elders of ___(church)___ encourages all Christians and non-Christians everywhere to humble themselves, seek God's forgiveness, and to repent of sinful attitudes and behavior. Then we have God's certain promise of remedy: He will hear our prayers, forgive our sins, and heal our land (2 Chronicles 7:14).

Revised 3/11/89

The above statement was written by Love & Action with the assistance of medical and legal advisers of the American Red Cross national headquarters, Washington, D.C.

For additional information and a list of books and teaching materials on AIDS ministry contact:

Love & Action
3 Church Circle #108
Annapolis, MD 21401
(410) 268-3442

187

We Resolve That . . .

During the summer of 1987 Calvin College and Seminary, Grand Rapids, Michigan, formed a task force on communicable disease to develop "an institutional response to the AIDS crisis." Its report includes a "pastoral statement" from which the following is excerpted:

God helping us, we resolve that we shall be a reformed Christian community of persons that:

1. *Flees what is sinful*
   A. Never shall we desert out of fear and disgust those who are stricken with AIDS.
   B. Never shall we resort to a censoriousness and persecution born of hate and individualism.
   C. Never shall we cherish and cultivate a judging spirit that spends more time on assessing fault than in ministering to the ill.
   D. Never shall we be unwilling to take Christ-like risks of help and compassion that might endanger our reputation, our good name, or our health, lest we be guilty of shunning and pharisaism.
   E. Never shall we be blithely smug and unconcerned.
   F. Never shall we cavalierly and easily assign a causal connection between sinful behavior and sad circumstances and illnesses.
   G. Never shall we exclude another out of pride.

2. *Does what is good*
   A. We shall identify with everyone who suffers, regardless of the cause.
   B. We shall strive to give the person with AIDS what he or she, like every other human being needs: understanding, acceptance, agapic love, trust, compassion, forgiveness, touch.
   C. We shall be guided by Christian compassion, prayer, and

the best judgments of medical science as we strive to determine whether or not the person with AIDS may continue to live and study within our community.

D. We shall pray faithfully with other Christians that our God will bring us a cure for this dreaded disease.

E. We shall be a community that encourages a "holy sexuality."

F. We shall continually affirm that sinful behavior does indeed have sad but predictable consequences.

Conclusion

The AIDS epidemic will force all of us to make hard choices, choices that reveal clearly what kind of people we are choosing to be. As many in smug and callous unconcern call for deserting and even persecuting the person with AIDS, let us resolve now to follow Jesus our Master, who willingly took risks, crossed barriers, touched lepers, met freely with the despised, took the blame, bore the stigma, and finally went "outside the camp" for us to bear our sins away.

Appendix D
Sample Funeral Service

Harlan Van Oort's Message at Scott's Memorial Service

Harlan began with this prayer:

> Almighty God whose love never fails and who can turn the shadow of death into the light of life, illumine us by your Spirit through your Word.
> We thank you for Scott, for the gift of his life, for the grace You have given him, for all in him that is good and kind and faithful. We thank You that, for him, death has passed and pain has ended and he has entered the joy You have prepared and the company of all saints.
> Give us faith to look beyond touch and sight, looking to Jesus our Savior and Lord, Amen.

Harlan then began his message this way:

> Scott's battle with AIDS and finally his death are difficult for me. I talked with college friends about the lack of sense life is making these days. The whys drift into the mysteries and they fill us with questions. But there is a final word from God in the fog. Jesus brings victory in the midst of mystery.
> My thoughts are mainly words from God. First a reading from 1 Corinthians 15.

> *Behold, I tell you a mystery: We shall not all sleep, but we shall all be changed—in a moment, in the twinkling of an eye, at the last trumpet. For the trumpet will sound, and the dead will be raised incorruptible, and we shall be changed. For this corruptible must put on incorruption, and this mortal must put on immortality. Then shall be brought to pass the saying that is written: "Death is swallowed up in victory."... But thanks be to God, who gives us the victory through our Lord Jesus Christ. (1 Cor. 15:51–54, 57)*

I first met Scott in college. We lived on the same wing. It seemed that wherever Scott went there was scrutiny and judgment. Being incredibly talented he received much evaluation. Every musical performance, every dramatic part usually received the highest kudos. Sometimes it didn't. There was judgment in other areas. Once Scott left his car parked overnight on a local street. It led us both into court, Scott as a defendant representing himself, and me as witness to the circumstances. And he won! He was in the middle of others' opinion, their prejudice, even judgment. Today I am grateful that Jesus has the last word on judgment.

A reading from Romans 8:

What then shall we say to these things? If God is for us, who can be against us? He who did not spare His own Son, but delivered Him up for us all, how shall He not with Him also freely give us all things? Who shall bring a charge against God's elect? It is God who justifies. Who is he who condemns? It is Christ who died, and furthermore is also risen, who is even at the right hand of God, who also makes intercession for us. Who shall separate us from the love of Christ? Shall tribulation, or distress, or persecution, or famine, or nakedness, or peril, or sword? As it is written:
"For Your sake we are killed all day long;
We are accounted as sheep for the slaughter."
Yet in all these things we are more than conquerors through Him who loved us. For I am persuaded that neither death nor life, nor angels nor principalities nor powers, nor things present nor things to come, nor height nor depth, nor any other created thing, shall be able to separate us from the love of God which is in Christ Jesus our Lord. (Rom. 8:31–39)

Scott struggled about belonging, where he fit in. Did he belong in college, this institution or that group, his home church, in a certain gay community, in his family, with his friends? Some of the places he tried to belong gave him trouble. Where is home? Scott struggled with that question. He even asked his parents, "Can I come home to die?" His family and this community's affirming answer was a testimony of Jesus' steadfast love. Ultimately Jesus has the last word for our destiny.

> *For we know that if our earthly house, this tent, is destroyed, we have a building from God, a house not made with hands, eternal in the heavens. . . . For we who are in this tent groan, being burdened, not because we want to be unclothed, but further clothed, that mortality may be swallowed up by life. Now He who has prepared us for this very thing is God, who also has given us the Spirit as a guarantee. (2 Cor. 5:1, 4–5)*

I think Scott is singing again today. Even in life he experienced God's eternal peace, and felt our Lord's forgiveness, but now he enjoys that everlasting Shalom with completeness and can sing Psalm 103 for all it's worth because our Lord has had His final word.

> *Bless the LORD, O my soul;*
> *And all that is within me, bless His holy name!*
> *Bless the LORD, O my soul,*
> *And forget not all His benefits:*
> *Who forgives all your iniquities,*
> *Who heals all your diseases,*
> *Who redeems your life from destruction,*
> *Who crowns you with lovingkindness and tender mercies,*
> *Who satisfies your mouth with good things,*
> *So that your youth is renewed like the eagle's.*
>
> *The LORD executes righteousness*
> *And justice for all who are oppressed. . . .*
> *The LORD is merciful and gracious,*
> *Slow to anger, and abounding in mercy.*

He will not always strive with us,
Nor will He keep His anger forever.
He has not dealt with us according to our sins,
Nor punished us according to our iniquities.

For as the heavens are high above the earth,
So great is His mercy toward those who fear Him;
As far as the east is from the west,
So far has He removed our transgressions from us.
As a father pities his children,
So the LORD pities those who fear Him.
For He knows our frame;
He remembers that we are dust. . . .

Bless the LORD, O my soul! (Ps. 103:1–6, 8–14, 22)

Appendix E
How to Start an HIV/AIDS Support Group

1. Recognize and realize the "need."
2. Choose a theme.
3. Find a trained facilitator, preferably someone who is HIV infected or affected and who has known the pain. The disease is your common bond.
4. Set up "Guidelines and Rules."
5. Decide on a time and place.
6. Publicize in newsletters, church bulletin boards, newspapers, talk radio, and by word of mouth.
7. Provide a "safe place" environment.
8. Provide confidentiality and mutual respect—essential for a successful group.
9. Pray and trust God to bless your efforts.

Notes

Chapter 4

1. Elisabeth Kübler-Ross, *On Death and Dying* (New York: Macmillan Publishing Co, Inc., 1969).

Chapter 5

1. AIDS Project Los Angeles, *AIDS: A Self-Care Manual* (Santa Monica, CA: IBS Press, 1987).

Chapter 6

1. Adapted from the booklet "On Dying, Death, and the Funeral" by Thomas P. Lynch (Milwaukee, WI: National Funeral Directors Association).

Chapter 8

1. "Fern Hill" by Dylan Thomas, from *The Poems of Dylan Thomas*. © 1945 by the trustees for the copyrights of Dylan Thomas. Reprinted by permission of New Directions Publishing Corp.

Chapter 11

1. For a more complete discussion of "The Seven Habits of Highly Effective Comforters," see my coauthor's book *How to Help a Heartbroken Friend* (Grand Rapids, MI: Revell, 1995), which applies Stephen R. Covey's *The 7 Habits of Highly Effective People* to the context of helping someone through heartbreak.
2. Stephen R. Covey, *The 7 Habits of Highly Effective People* (New York: Simon & Schuster, 1989), 262–263.

Chapter 13

1. Barbara E. Johnson, *Where Does a Mother Go to Resign?* (Minneapolis, MN: Bethany House, 1979).

About the Authors

Mignon Zylstra and her husband, Bob, cofounded *Support for the Journey,* a non-profit organization for HIV infected people and their loved ones. When not working one-on-one with people affected by HIV, she speaks throughout the United States on the need for physical, emotional, and spiritual support for those living with HIV/AIDS. The Zylstras live in Oak Harbor, Washington. They have two married daughters and three grandchildren.

David B. Biebel earned his Doctor of Ministry degree in Personal Wholeness in 1986 from Gordon-Conwell Theological Seminary in South Hamilton, Massachusetts. He is ordained with the Evangelical Free Church of America. He has authored or coauthored nine other books including *Jonathan, You Left Too Soon; If God Is So Good, Why Do I Hurt So Bad?;* and *How to Help a Heartbroken Friend.*

****

For more information about *Support for the Journey,* write:

Support for the Journey
P.O. Box 1794
Oak Harbor, WA 98277